The Kinks Are

The Village Green

Preservation Society

Also available in this series:

Forthcoming in this series:

The Kinks Are
The Village Green
Preservation Society

Andy Miller

continuum
NEW YORK • LONDON

2006

The Continuum International Publishing Group Inc
80 Maiden Lane, New York, NY 10038

The Continuum International Publishing Group Ltd
The Tower Building, 11 York Road, London SE1 7NX

www.continuumbooks.com

Printed in the United States of America

Library of Congress Cataloging-in-Publication Data

Miller, Andy.
The Kinks are the Village Green Preservation Society /
Andy Miller.
p. cm. — (33 1/3)
Includes bibliographical references (p.) and discography (p.).

ISBN 0-8264-1498-2 (pbk. : alk. paper)
1. Davies, Ray, 1944- Kinks are the Village
Green Preservation Society.
2. Kinks (Musical group) I. Title. II. Series
ML420.D25M55 2003
781.42166'092'2—dc21
2003011466

Contents

Acknowledgements

This book could not have been written without the considerable help of the following people:

Keith Altham, Mick Avory, Louis Barfe, Nicola Barker, Michael Bracewell, Alex Clark, John Dalton, Peter Doggett, Dave Emlen, Jonny Geller, Clinton Heylin, Philip Hoare, Jim Irvin, Michael Keane, Tony Lacey, Stewart Lee, Shawn Levy, Linda McBride at Konk, Bill Orton, Pete Quaife, Dan Rhodes, Andrew Sandoval, Klaus Schmalenbach, Russell Smith, Ben Thompson, Jerome Wallerstein, Simon Wells, Barric Wentzell, Paul Wright.

In particular I would like to thank Doug Hinman for his enthusiasm and readiness to help with any enquiry, and Jon Savage, for giving me access to transcripts of the interviews he conducted with Ray Davies for *The Kinks, The Official Biography*.

At Continuum, David Barker for commissioning the book in the first place, and all his subsequent encouragement.

Most importantly, special thanks to my wife Tina for her love, support and continuing willingness to listen to The Kinks, and to me.

The Official Kinks Fan Club can be reached at PO Box 30, Atherstone, Warwickshire, CV9 2ZX, United Kingdom, or on the web via http://kinks.it.rit.edu/.

For M.F., M.K., P.W.

Modern nostalgia is a mourning for the impossibility of mythical return, for the loss of an enchanted world with clear borders and values; it could be a secular expression of a spiritual longing, a nostalgia for an absolute, a home that is both physical and spiritual, the edenic unity of time and space before entry into history. The nostalgic is looking for a spiritual addressee. Encountering silence, he looks for memorable signs, desperately misreading them.

The Future of Nostalgia, Svetlana Boym, 2001

"If I could live over again I'd change every single thing I've ever done."[i]

Ray Davies, November 1967

Chapter One — The Boy Next Door, Only Better

In July 1966, *Disc and Music Echo* magazine invited Ray Davies to review *Revolver*, the new album by The Beatles. It was a canny choice. The Kinks' 'Sunny Afternoon' had recently knocked The Beatles' 'Paperback Writer' off the top of the hit parade after just one week, an event Davies would subsequently describe as "one of the joys of my life".[ii] It confirmed The Kinks in their position as court jesters to the new pop aristocracy — "those brilliant piss-takers," as George Melly called them — a part of the Carnebetian army and apart from it also. The exalted young composer, with his beautiful wife and baby daughter, sat in his residence up in leafy Muswell Hill and surveyed the city scene with detached amusement. "I had achieved everything I had set out to do creatively and I was twenty-two years old," Davies later wrote.[iii] At the end of the month, the England football team beat Germany and won the World Cup. London was swinging and Ray Davies was in heaven.

Sure enough, Davies' verdict on *Revolver* was characteristically irreverent — to modern eyes, his comments seem like sacrilege. 'Yellow Submarine' was "a load of rubbish". 'Eleanor Rigby' "sounds like they're out to please music teachers in primary schools." 'Here, There And Everywhere' proved merely that "the Beatles have got good memories, because there are a lot of busy chords in it." And as for 'Tomorrow Never Knows' . . . "Listen to all those crazy sounds!" exclaimed *Disc*'s guest critic. "I can imagine they had George Martin tied to a totem pole when they did this."

"This is the first Beatles LP I've really listened to in its entirety, but I must say there are better songs on *Rubber Soul*," Davies concluded, gleefully contradicting himself. He then delivered one final sliver of faint praise. "I don't want to be harsh . . . the balance and recording technique are as good as ever."[iv]

Although he feigned a distance from his contemporaries, in reality Ray Davies kept a keen eye on their successes — and failures. "Sometimes the rivals are closer to you in life than the friends," he said.[v] Among those he paid particular attention to were The Beatles and The Who. "Townshend was very competitive," Davies recalled in 1988. "Paul McCartney was one of the most competitive people I've ever met. Lennon wasn't. He just thought everyone else was shit."[vi]

With the benefit of hindsight, two of Davies' remarks about *Revolver* stand out. Of the Indian sound of George Harrison's 'Love You To', he observes, "This sort of song I was doing two years ago — now I'm doing what the Beatles were doing two years ago." With the guitar drone of their 1965 single 'See My Friends', The Kinks had anticipated the vogue for 'raga rock', as practised by The Beatles, The Byrds and The Rolling Stones. By mid-1966, however, Davies seemingly wanted to reach back to a pre-experimental Beatles — to a whole pre-experimental pop music that incorporated elements of jazz and music hall — an impression confirmed by what he had to say about 'Good Day Sunshine': "This is back to the real old Beatles. I just don't like the electronic stuff. The Beatles were supposed to be like the boy next door only better."[vii]

The boy next door only better — it could be a description of Ray Davies. For the obstreperous Kinks frontman, 'I'm Not Like Everybody Else' was more than just a boast, it was a modus operandi. "Most people think from a business point of view, 'Well, that's popular, we'll do that,'" says Mick Avory, The Kinks' drummer through the 1960's and beyond. "But Ray never thinks like that. He thinks, 'What can I do that's not going to follow their trend?' And that's where he goes next." In summer 1966, while all around was experimentation with tape loops, phasing, backwards guitars — the atmospheric interference of the gathering psychedelic storm — Davies was concentrating on songwriting craft. 'Sunny Afternoon' was the first manifestation of a new signature Kinks style that would culminate two years later in *The Kinks Are The Village Green Preservation Society*. But by then, few people were listening.

After several delays, track revisions and some last-ditch recording sessions, *The Kinks Are The Village Green Preservation Society* (hereafter known as *TKATVGPS*) was released in the UK on November 22nd 1968, coincidentally the same date The Beatles released their new double LP set, *The Beatles* a.k.a. 'The White Album'. Two years on, the close-run rivalries of 1966 were ancient history. Worldwide, The Beatles sold two million copies of their album in a week, and were once again hailed from pop paper to broadsheet as the most splendid avatars of the age. The Kinks, meanwhile, were mostly forgotten or ignored. *TKATVGPS* charted nowhere in the world; the combined US sales of the album and its predecessor *Something Else By The Kinks* were estimated at a paltry 25,000. The Who, meanwhile, were readying *Tommy*, the blockbusting concept LP that would seal their reputation as rock's heaviest innovators. Banned from performing in America, supposedly for offensive behaviour, The Kinks could only watch as their hellraising rivals marched on without them. It was an embarrassment for a group who, just a year earlier, could still be relied upon to sell 200,000 singles with every release, and whose chief songwriter was routinely feted as pop's most sparkling auteur. The humiliation was compounded by an awareness among the handful of people that got to hear it that, in *TKATVGPS*, Ray Davies had produced his best work to date.

The Kinks' new album wilfully disregarded anything fashionable in British rock or pop at the time. There were no long guitar solos, no extended freeform jams, no lyrics based on the Tibetan *Book Of The Dead* or *The Communist Manifesto*. Instead, The Kinks "were singing songs about lost friends, draught beer, motorbike riders, wicked witches and flying cats," as Davies wrote in his autobiography *X-Ray*.[viii] He drew on a well of personal and traditional sources to create an album which, although nominally concerned with the characters that live around a village green, goes deep into territory rarely explored in pop: memory, regret, failure, growing old. The record sounds very English, but its Englishness is a sideshow, a metaphor for the universal problem Davies was wrestling with — the problem of being alive.

These days, *TKATVGPS* is widely acknowledged as the high point of Ray Davies' often confounding career, a turn of events he seems to find both gratifying and infuriating, ruefully referring to the album both as his favourite Kinks album and "the most acclaimed flop of all time . . . I mean, even the people who talk about it, haven't heard it."[ix] To Jon Savage, he was brusque in his assessment. "There were two points in my life, in my career, when I should not have been allowed to put records out: then and in 1973 to 1975 . . . It's a very intimate album. That's the problem. Paul Schrader once said to me, 'When you get a good story, you get a personal problem, then you turn it into a metaphor.' I didn't do that. I just got the personal problem. But in a way *Village Green* is a metaphor. I still listen to it, and it's still the most durable record from that period."[x]

Davies' mixed emotions about the album stem from the circumstances in which he made it. For two years, he worked on *TKATVGPS* as a potential stage presentation, then a solo project, then as a new Kinks record. The group stockpiled enough wonderful music for two albums, much of which remains officially unavailable. As the pop climate shifted around him and The Kinks' fortunes waned, he persevered. The LP's line-up went from twelve tracks to twenty to fifteen. And when Davies' pet project was finally released it flopped. Worse, it was ignored. The group's profile on the pop scene was minimal and The Kinks' label, Pye Records, was a singles-based outfit that had yet to adapt to the switch to albums that had occurred in the wake of *Sgt. Pepper's*

Lonely Hearts Club Band. So in late 1968, no one knew Ray Davies had just painted his masterpiece — small wonder he regards its belated elevation to cult status with scepticism.

For the other members of The Kinks, the LP is more straightforwardly special. Dave Davies calls it "a very beautiful record".[xi] "It was more of a band effort," says Mick Avory. "It was collaborative, rather than him writing a song and going in like session men and just doing it." Bassist Pete Quaife, who would leave the group a few months after the album's release, agrees. "This is what made it unique," he says. "When we made that LP all of us managed to get in ideas and put them over and do them, which was amazing. It's the best album we made. I know I played on the damn thing, but every time I listen to it I think — this is worth something, this album. It really is." Thousands of people all over the world — who, *pace* Ray Davies, have actually heard it — would agree.

In the time it took to make *TKATVGPS*, The Kinks dropped off the pop radar. They were yesterday's men, an identity the ever-contrary Ray Davies seemed to embrace on his instantly out-of-date new album. "I think the fashion in music was probably a bit different," says Mick Avory with knowing understatement. "That was The Kinks — always trying to set a trend ahead of its time!"

The Kinks Are The Village Green Preservation Society is not just the best album The Kinks ever made, but as the years have passed since its release, it stands revealed as the only album of the pop era to look beyond the 1960s and consider what might happen next. This is the story of how, by conspicuously failing to set a trend, The Kinks created something enduring and unsurpassed, not just the most perfect manifestation of Ray Davies' inimitable wit, sadness, quiet anger and charm, but also a timeless reminder that every party, however fabulous, has to come to an end.

*   *   *

Back in 1966, The Kinks followed 'Sunny Afternoon' with their first great album *Face To Face* and another classic single, 'Dead End Street', whose descending bass figure and kitchen-sink drama scenario made it a minor key reprise of 'Sunny Afternoon'. For the first time, The Kinks revealed their full range as an ensemble. The LP showcased the new facets of Davies' writing — vulnerability ('Fancy', 'Too Much On My Mind'), the importance of family ('Rosie Won't You Please Come Home'), mores of money and class ('A House In The Country', 'Most Exclusive Residence For Sale'), as well as the aforementioned brilliant piss-taking ('Dandy', 'Session Man'). Although not specifically written about him, this last song has become synonymous with Nicky Hopkins, the shy young keyboard player featured prominently on *Face To Face*, whose distinctive piano and harpsichord parts would do much to define The Kinks' sound for the next two years. "He was the kid at school that everybody liked. He could pick up a song up practically before it had been played," recalls Pete Quaife fondly. "And it would be exactly what was wanted. Exactly! It was wonderful to watch."

Face To Face was recorded bit by bit between October 1965 and June 1966. Davies had originally planned to link the tracks with sound effects, some of which survive on the finished LP — the waves at the beginning of 'Holiday In Waikiki', Kinks' manager Grenville Collins answering the phone on 'Party Line'. However, Pye Records objected to such self-indulgence and Davies was required to rework the album, editing some of the sound effects and dropping some tracks ('End Of The Season', possibly 'Big Black Smoke'). It set an ominous precedent for the protracted gestation and forcible alteration of *TKATVGPS*.

Face To Face was a commercial success, but the idea of creating a more sophisticated, interlinked piece of work still preoccupied Ray Davies. "I wasn't too keen on the last LP," he said in February 1967. "It was more of a collection of songs than an LP, it didn't seem to fit together too well."[xii] In the studio, he continued to push The Kinks forward, employing an arranger to score light orchestral accompaniment on 'Two Sisters' and a new song Davies had high hopes for — 'Village Green'.

However, although Davies was on a creative winning streak, all was not well. The previous year, the pressures of touring and promotional work had driven him to a nervous breakdown. The earnings from his songwriting were being held in escrow while an acrimonious legal suit between Davies and The Kinks' former management/publishing team of Larry Page and Eddie Kassner dragged on through the courts (the case would go as far as the House of Lords, and would not be resolved until October 1968). He felt increasingly constricted by the machinery of the pop business, the relentless demand for new product, while being simultaneously frustrated by The Kinks' enforced exile from the USA. Furthermore, Davies' insistence on following his own musical path was creating divisions within The Kinks, never the most harmonious group in the first place. "I think that Pete and Dave are happier playing rock'n'roll. Mick and I seem to prefer the kind of thing we're doing now," he told *Record Mirror*. "I can't see us changing the type of song we're recording at the moment. We've only had a few singles out on those lines and there's plenty of scope."[xiii]

The sessions for what would become *Something Else By The Kinks* continued through the spring of 1967. In the course of these recordings, the relationship between The Kinks and producer Shel Talmy came to an end, leaving Ray Davies as the group's sole leader in the studio. There is some dispute over who produced what in this period — both men claim the perfect 'Waterloo Sunset' is his recording alone — but Davies subsequently bemoaned the lack of an outside influence on both *Something Else* and *TKATVGPS*. "I'd come off producing those hits, three or four hits, so they thought, 'Oh let him do it'," he told Jon Savage. "Probably I wouldn't have listened to anybody else but they could have been a better production."[xiv] At the time however, Davies relished this new freedom.

The week after the release of the widely acclaimed and chart bound 'Waterloo Sunset', a shock headline appeared in *New Musical Express*: RAY DAVIES QUITTING KINKS? Davies, it was reported, was considering following the example of The Beach Boys' Brian Wilson, who had renounced touring to concentrate on his group's music.

"A substitute will have to take my place," said Davies. "There just isn't enough time for me to make personal appearances and work on the Kinks' records. On Wednesday, for instance, I have to leave on our Scandinavian tour in the middle of my work. This kind of situation hinders my songwriting activities, and it's also obviously a handicap to the group. I still intend to sing on the Kinks' records, because my work is written around the group. There is no question of my severing all connection with them. It's possible I may also undertake work of an individual nature, as long as it does not conflict with my interests with the Kinks."[xv]

The Kinks' management rushed to limit the damage (while no doubt enjoying the publicity for the new single). Robert Wace was quoted thus: "There is no truth in it at all. These rumours are being put around by people with some sort of axe to grind,"[xvi] ignoring the fact that the principal axeman was Davies himself. The following Tuesday, an apparently abashed Ray Davies telephoned *NME*. "I am lead singer," he said. "It is difficult to find a substitute for a lead singer. So I will appear on all Kinks shows."[xvii]

Years later, Davies recalled the circumstances surrounding this flurry of activity.

> "I went out with Grenville and Robert, my managers then, and I said 'Look, I've done 'Waterloo Sunset', what more do you want? I've done all these records — singles — and I want to do something else.' And they said, 'Well old boy, just keep giving us the singles and we'll see if anything comes along.' "[xviii]

Concurrently, Davies and The Kinks' management saw the potential of Dave Davies as that very thing. The younger brother was already the group's pin-up; "I feel I should exploit him more," said Ray.[xix] After the top five success of his single 'Death Of A Clown' in August 1967, a fully-fledged Dave Davies solo career was mooted, something The Kinks' raver-in-chief seemed happy to go along with. "Dave has contemporary features and an enormous following amongst the girls," was his brother's assessment. "There's no reason why he should not become a very big solo name."[xx] "The plan is for Dave to do numbers with some of that early Kinks excitement and thus allow The Kinks to become more sophisticated as a group," said Robert Wace.[xxi] And, presumably, to create some space for Ray Davies to work on his solo project and simultaneously keep the hits coming.

Through the spring and summer of 1967, Davies considered the form this solo piece would take. His ambitions seemed limitless. Press reports of the time speak of "a solo LP with an orchestra and things like that"[xxii], "my own LP of ideas and songs"[xxiii], "a solo LP with the songs linked up in a musical story"[xxiv], an album of songs about London, an adaptation of Dylan Thomas' *Under Milk Wood*, maybe a theatrical presentation. . . . One of the tracks was reported to be called

'Hole In The Sock Of', "a good-humoured swipe at 'A Day In The Life' on the Beatles LP" (those damn Beatles again). Bar the last, all these elements would find a home in *TKATVGPS*.[1]

"Well, I was kind of bored with what I was doing," said Ray Davies in the mid-1980s, referring to the circuitous route to *TKATVGPS*. "And just looking back now, I should . . . It would have been a good time to abandon — not abandon, but to call a halt to the band for a bit. Because Dave was doing quite well, and his solo stuff was accepted, and I should have gone off and done other things."[xxv] It was a regret he reiterated in 2003. "I should have left the band to do that record. That could have been the start of my solo career."[xxvi]

But in 1967, there was no pressing need for Davies to go solo — as long as The Kinks, and now Dave Davies, remained at the top, there was time for any or all of these schemes to reach fruition. The release of the uplifting, multi-layered 'Autumn Almanac' in October, another top five hit, seemed to confirm their unassail-

---

[1]So prevalent were reports of Kinks solo projects, that an irritated Dave Davies started making a joke of it. "Pete is doing 'Flight of the Bumble bee' on his bass and there is an album coming out called 'Mick Avory Plays Buddy Rich'!" he told *NME*. ("He smiled that smile of acute agony, which is so characteristic of brother Ray," observed Keith Altham, *NME*, July 15th 1967).

able position. There was talk of a Kinks television series, even a film.

However, in retrospect, 'Autumn Almanac' marked the first hint of trouble for The Kinks. This glorious single, one of the greatest achievements of British 60's pop, was widely criticised at the time for being too similar to previous Davies efforts. "Is it time Ray stopped writing about gray suburbanites going about their fairly unemotional daily business?" asked Nick Jones in *Melody Maker*. "One feels Ray works to a formula, not a feeling, and it's becoming boring."[xxvii] Some Radio One DJs were of a like mind. "Since 'Dead End Street' Ray Davies seems to have been in a musical rut, and it's time he tried something different," opined Johnnie Walker, while Mike Ahern was less diplomatic: "A load of old rubbish — a nothing record which wouldn't have meant a light if anyone else had recorded it."[xxviii] Unthinkably, it would be three years before The Kinks again breached the top ten.

There were other ill omens for the group. The new Kinks LP *Something Else By The Kinks* had been issued in September 1967. It should have been a triumph but, although it contained some of Davies' most deathless and varied work ('David Watts', 'Two Sisters', 'No Return'), the LP was almost too diffuse, and sounded less coherent than *Face To Face*. In addition, next to "big statements" like *Sgt. Pepper* . . . , Davies' idiosyncratic vignettes suddenly appeared small and inconsequential. Thirty-five years later, we treasure them as examples of Davies at the peak of his powers; then, modest songs about cigarettes, afternoon tea and tin soldiers seemed to bespeak a fatal lack of ambition. Consequently, *Something Else By The Kinks* failed to sell. Pye's habit of issuing budget Kinks collections on their Marble Arch label cannot have helped — just eight weeks after *Something Else . . .* hit the shops, *Sunny Afternoon* appeared, containing the eponymous hit single, 'Dedicated Follower Of Fashion' and 'Dead End Street'. As the market shifted towards albums, The Kinks were still primarily seen as singles act, and rather than take a chance on an expensive new LP, people preferred to buy the old hits cheap. New Kinks' singles, meanwhile, were starting to struggle. Despite a big promotional push, Dave Davies' follow-up to 'Death Of A Clown', the bawdy 'Susannah's Still Alive', sold a humbling 59,000 copies, and failed to make the top ten in November.

By the end of the year, The Kinks were rapidly sliding out of fashion. They were increasingly thought of as an anachronism, a throwback to the beat boom. How did Ray Davies respond to these warning signs? By burying his head in his work, doggedly pursuing his vision, or visions, for new records for himself and his group. As Christmas 1967 came and went, down in the basement of Pye Records, The Kinks carried on recording, recording, recording . . .

*   *   *

Ray Davies wrote nearly all the songs for *TKATVGPS* in the living room of his white Georgian house at 87 Fortis Green, North London.[2] He and Dave had grown up just a few hundred yards away, in a small semi-detached at 6 Denmark Terrace. Nearby stand houses whose names are synonymous with a historical Englishness — Albion Lodge, Trafalgar Cottage, a timber-beamed health club called The Manor. "Our neighbourhood was like a village," Davies said recently. "That part of London is still magical."[xxix] In his childhood

---

[2] In *X-Ray*, Davies records that before writing *TKATVGPS*, he, Rasa and Louisa "had taken up residence in a manorial mock Tudor mansion in Elstree." "As soon as I moved into that house I wasn't really happy," he told Jon Savage, a story that has passed into Kinks folklore. In fact, Davies did not move from Fortis Green to Borehamwood until August 1968, by which time the vast majority of *TKATVGPS* had been both written and recorded. In the depressing environment of his new house, the failure of *TKATVGPS* no doubt fresh in his mind, Davies started work on 'Plastic Man' and *Arthur*. The Davies family, now with their second daughter Victoria, soon moved back to Fortis Green.

stamping ground, with Highgate nearby, and Hampstead Heath stretching down to Archway, Davies did not have to look far for inspiration for his imaginary village green.

Throughout the period of The Kinks' greatest success, Ray Davies kept his family close around him, and family was a theme that bubbled to the surface of *TKATVGPS*. "I think on *The Village Green* they were all brothers and sisters," he told Jonathan Cott. "Nobody made love because it was all in the family. I don't think there's a love song on it."[xxx] "A big thing that really helped Ray and I and the Kinks was our family, in the time when people were talking about rebelling against absolutely everything," Dave Davies said in 2001.[xxxi]

Ray Davies acknowledges his family's influence on the way he wrote and presented his work. "Growing up in that family, it had a strong musical basis. They were not great musicians, but music was very much part of the family, and we always had to sing songs at the piano. That really undoubtedly rubbed off on me. Things that my father saw, the family knew. I never went to the music hall, or any of that stuff. He went to see musical shows and used to go dancing, so I picked up a lot of it from my family."[xxxii] It is no coincidence that many Kinks tracks from this era, such as 'Autumn Almanac', 'Wonderboy' and 'People Take Pictures Of Each

Other', feature sing-a-longs that owe as much to family get-togethers as they do to the music hall tradition.

Accordingly, throughout the 1960's, The Kinks — who Davies wryly calls "another family to me, however dysfunctional that family can be sometimes"[xxxiii] — would rehearse in the manner of the Davies clan, gathered round the piano in Ray's front room while he led them through his latest composition.

Dave Davies: "All the good stuff happened like that. The phone would ring and Ray would say, 'Dave, come around, I've got this idea'. I'd get in the car, walk in the house, Rasa would make a cup of tea. He'd say 'What do you think of this?' . . . You listen to 'Sunny Afternoon' and you can see the light coming through the curtains in the morning, it's got that kind of magic to it because that's what it was like. It was like Ray's front room."[xxxiv]

Because he rarely made demos of his songs to give to other members of the group, arrangements would be worked up at Davies' house. Mick Avory had a special practice drum kit made from foam pads so as not to annoy the neighbours. "We'd have to pick the songs up by ear," remembers Pete Quaife. "Ray would say, 'This is in D', and we would run through it a couple of times. He'd go 'You got it?' and we'd go, 'Yeah, we got it.' 'OK, next number,' and that's how it went. And then a few days later you'd get down into the studio and you'd play *exactly* what you played at Ray's house."

Mick Avory: "We used to jam sometimes, and Ray would get the feeling of what the band was good at playing together and he could work it into the song. You might come up with some idea and he'd say 'That's good!' and maybe polish it a bit more. He'd record things for himself on his little cassette player and then listen back to them when he was sat down at the piano writing again. He wouldn't always have completely written the song. He might have written the words or the basic idea, but he wanted to make it sound like the band."

By the time The Kinks started work on *TKATVGPS*, Davies had developed the habit of rehearsing and recording songs without sharing the lyrics or melody line with the rest of the group. Mick Avory puts this quirk down to justifiable paranoia ("Ray didn't trust everyone with hearing the song. . . . Sometimes things got stolen. It has happened,"), while Quaife attributes it to "Ray playing silly buggers. That's the way he was and you just had to accept it." However, both admit that it made life complicated when it came to interpreting new material.

"It drove me *nuts*," says Quaife. "You wanted to know where the melody was going, so you could run up, run down, introduce the major part of the number, and so on." Avory agrees. "In his songs, Ray doesn't always repeat things in a logical fashion. It's much better if you've got the vocal, because then you can do fills and embellishments that don't get in the way of it. Sometimes you'd listen to the finished track and just think, 'Ugh! Shouldn't have done that!' "

The majority of Kinks' recording sessions took place in Pye Studio 2, the smaller of the two studios in the basement of the Pye Records offices at Marble Arch. Behind the four-track recording console were Pye's in-house engineers Brian Humphries and Alan Mackenzie ('Mac' for short). "They were affable, very open," says Pete Quaife, "but I don't recall them contributing ideas. They were there to make sure the needles didn't go into the red."

Although Pye was well equipped for the time, it was a small and not particularly luxurious environment. "It was very dark," remembers Quaife. "The walls were a very dull kind of dark brown colour. There was a carpet on the floor, which had cigarette burns everywhere. You couldn't really see the ceiling because it was the same colour as tobacco."

"They didn't go out of their way to make it look comfortable or give it any sort of atmosphere," observes Mick Avory, who has helped run Konk Studios for twenty years. "They wanted it done fairly quickly as well. You couldn't spend too long in there. The Beatles could lock out EMI for three months and that was it, they could live, eat and sleep in there. But Pye wasn't EMI, and we weren't The Beatles." The Kinks would grab studio time when it was available, "especially late afternoon and during the night," says Quaife. "That's why we all look so sleepy in photographs, with tobacco tans."

As a general rule, The Kinks would lay down a rhythm track first, consisting of drums, bass and Davies on piano or rhythm guitar. Avory would be recorded with two microphones over the kit, plus microphones on his bass and snare drums, while Quaife's Rickenbacker bass was plugged straight into the desk. Other instrumentation would then be added — percussion, Dave Davies' guitar parts or assorted keyboards from Ray Davies or Nicky Hopkins.

It was Davies' practice to run through multiple takes of songs. "When Shel left, that's when we started working more in that way and the group had more opportunity to flesh out the sound," says Mick Avory, although he acknowledges the democratic process had a patent cut-off point. "Everyone had different ideas about the way we should go, but Ray was the one that was steering the ship, so he was the one you had to go with." Band members not contributing were still required to be present throughout recording sessions. "He'd keep you there for hours," grumbles Pete Quaife, "and he wouldn't let you out of the studio either. You'd have to be there even though you weren't doing anything."

With the instrumental tracks complete, the results would be mixed down and vocals added. The Kinks' accomplished harmonies sound all the more impressive when one realises the arrangements were usually worked out on the spot. As is well known, the group's vocal blend was often augmented with Rasa Davies' distinctively wispy falsetto but, according to Pete Quaife, Rasa also acted as a go-between for her husband. "She'd keep peace in the group just by being there. She'd come down into the studio and say 'Could you try this or that?' And because she was a nice little nineteen-year old girl, you'd say, 'Well, OK, yeah'," he laughs.

So it was that, through a mix of guile, persuasion and control, Davies shepherded his songs from the front room in Fortis Green to the recording studio and onto tape, keeping it in the family every step of the way. Outside, meanwhile, the world kept going round.

*   *   *

The Kinks' disastrous 1968 began with the release in January of a live LP, *Live At Kelvin Hall*. It was the third Kinks album Pye had issued in a little under four months, a scream-saturated dash through a few old hits and an unlikely medley combining 'Milk Cow Blues', 'Tired Of Waiting For You' and the theme from *Batman*. The record did nothing to dispel the group's increasingly outdated image. Sales were negligible.[3]

Ironically, live work or the lack of it, would loom large in the months ahead. After his breakdown, Ray Davies cut back the number of concert engagements he was willing to undertake, preferring to concentrate his energies in the recording studio. The other members of The Kinks were frequently left at a loose end. In interviews, Dave Davies presented his continuing dalliance with a solo career as a way of occupying himself. "The Kinks, let's face it, are not the busiest group in the business," he told Bob Farmer in February. "Much of the time we sit at home while Ray writes his songs and as we don't work all that much I felt that I might as well spend my plentiful spare time promoting my solo career . . . I enjoy working instead of just sitting around doing nothing . . . "[xxxv]

"We weren't doing much gigging," says Mick Avory today. "The band did come quite close to splitting up. I left at least twice, just through frustration really. We

---

[3]*Live At Kelvin Hall* is perhaps not as live as all that. Sessions were undertaken to "sweeten" the original tapes. Close listening seems to reveal that the audience hysteria is an extended, repeating tape loop.

weren't working enough and we weren't making the money. I always felt we should be out there doing it. Instead, we were lying around doing nothing basically — to a large extent that's the way Ray wanted it."

So the news that The Kinks had been booked on a coffer-replenishing month-long package tour of provincial Granadas and ABCs must have caused Davies' heart to sink. Throughout April, from Mansfield to Bournemouth, via Cardiff, Chester and Slough, The Kinks would be sharing a stage with The Herd, The Tremeloes, Gary Walker and the Rain, and Sweden's finest, Ola and the Janglers. On the burgeoning rock scene, these concerts were considered old-fashioned and lightweight, jamborees where teenagers came to scream rather than listen. The gap between Davies' ambition and his group's public profile was growing ever wider.

Davies spent the winter prior to the tour writing songs for a weekly late-night television show, *At The Eleventh Hour* (see 'The Village Green Preservation Society', p. 50) and accumulating new Kinks tracks, many of which prominently featured a Mellotron Mk2. Davies had become enamoured of the bulky, tape-operated instrument, a precursor to the synthesiser, after a visit to Graham Nash's house in May 1967. It offered a cheap alternative to the real string and brass sections Davies wanted to use on his new recordings, but which Pye was reluctant to fund. In addition, the Mellotron, played by Nicky Hopkins or Davies himself, gave Davies autonomy over the arrangements of his songs.

These fresh Kinks recordings, including 'Mr. Songbird', 'Phenomenal Cat', 'Berkeley Mews' and 'Wonderboy', had more in common than a new-fangled musical instrument. Although their eventual fate was uncertain — a Kinks' LP, single, Davies' solo project or whatever — there was a connection between them and other, newer tracks Davies was working on, suggested in part by 'Village Green', the Bach-inspired song The Kinks had recorded a year earlier. Davies had kept that recording in the tape vault, close to his heart. Now he was beginning to create a setting for his pastoral verse to be heard — character sketches like 'Do You Remember Walter', 'Monica' and 'Johnny Thunder', and a trilogy of songs about memory, 'Picture Book', 'Pictures In The Sand' and 'People Take Pictures Of Each Other'. Some numbers stuck closely to a Village Green theme, others less so, but the shared sensibility of these new compositions was their author's preoccupation with the past. The Kinks' leader seemed to be mourning a loss of innocence, personal and national, in song. Davies felt trapped by the group, trapped by Britain and trapped in his marriage, embroiled in an extramarital affair. He felt old. Above all, these new

Davies songs articulated their author's yearning to be somewhere else.

Once the April tour got under way, Davies' unhappiness was evident in his on-stage demeanour. "Ray seemed a bit bored by the whole business — his 'sad clown' face forcing the occasional toothy grin to convince us he was really having a ball," reported *Disc and Music Echo* from Walthamstow on the second date of the tour. Night after night, The Kinks ran through a desultory set, which included 'Sunny Afternoon', 'Death Of A Clown' and their new single 'Wonderboy'. "It was a chore, very dull, boring and straightforward," says Pete Quaife. "We only did twenty minutes, but it used to drive me absolutely frantic, standing on stage playing three notes over and over again."

As the tour progressed, tickets stubbornly refused to sell. Venues were sometimes only half-full. Those who did buy tickets largely came to scream at The Herd whose singer Peter Frampton had been marketed as 'the Face of 68'. In general, the teenyboppers were not there to see the boring old Kinks, who occasionally had to endure chants of "We Want The Herd!" during their brief appearances.

"In 68 and 69 it was very difficult. People laughed at you if you said you were a Kinks' fan," remembers Bill Orton, president of the Kinks Fan Club, who was fourteen when he saw the group for the first time in Coventry, on the tour's last night. "I went to the early show. My seat was in the third row, so I had some screaming girls next to me. They were looking at the bill and saying, 'Well, there's nobody here except The Herd'. In fact, whatever band came on they went crazy anyway." Although Bill enjoyed the concert, he was surprised at the group's perfunctory treatment of their biggest hit 'You Really Got Me'. "At the end of the show, the curtain came down, they played the opening riff, and then didn't carry on. That was it."

The mood of despondency engendered by the tour was not improved by the abject failure of 'Wonderboy', "a flop staggering in its finality and completeness," as Chris Welch wrote a few months later. "It was put out because we were going on tour," said Davies. "We had made that title as an album track, but they wanted to take it out as a single while we were on tour. But I was not too sure of its single potential."[xxxvi] He was right. The track was a mess, one of Davies' finest lyrics hidden beneath a trite arrangement and murky production. It sold 27,000 copies, a tenth of 'Waterloo Sunset' or 'Autumn Almanac', and barely crawled into the top forty.

For Pete Quaife, 'Wonderboy' crystallised the mounting dissatisfaction he felt with The Kinks. " 'Wonderboy' was horrible," he says. "It sounded like

Herman's Hermits wanking. Jesus, it was bad. I hated it. I remember recording it and doing the la-la-las and just thinking, 'What kind of bloody prissy sissy nonsense are we doing? We're the guys that made "You Really Got Me", for Chrissakes!' "

"What really pissed me off is that we were pandering to what Ray wanted to be, how he wanted to be perceived. It was very much a Noël Coward kind of idea, and we were being forced to go along with it. I felt quite stupid doing it, to be honest. I don't really blame Ray, I blame the managers for putting thoughts into his head, telling him he could do this and he could do that, without giving any regard to the other members of the group."

Quaife had known Davies since school, and it infuriated him to see Ray receive what he considered preferential treatment. Mick Avory, however, was a latecomer to the band and took a more sanguine view. "When it came down to it, the management knew they had to look after Ray and pamper him," he says. "He was the main writer in the band, he wrote all the hits. The rest of the group were just there. From more or less being all the same when you first start, Ray comes out of the group and he's on a pedestal — but that's through his talent, rather than someone just putting him there. I mean, Pete Quaife's got a certain amount of talent, but he ain't got Ray's talent, and neither has Dave. It's no good me saying we should all be the same — we ain't the same."

The dual flops of the April tour and 'Wonderboy' hit The Kinks hard. To Pete Quaife in particular, they confirmed that Ray Davies' domination of the group, encouraged by a shortsighted management team, was smothering The Kinks and bringing their career to a speedy close. For Davies himself the race was now on to get his Village Green album completed and released the way he wanted it, while The Kinks still retained their commercial clout. The previous year's dreams of a Ray Davies solo project began to fade.

The Kinks returned to the studio in May to add to their cache of inspired recordings: 'Picture Book', 'Animal Farm', 'Johnny Thunder' and the superb 'Days'. At this stage, Davies seems not to have had the album's contents worked out beyond his initial Village Green idea — *TKATVGPS*, a subtly different and more sophisticated creation, was still some way off. Typically, he did not discuss it much with the other members of The Kinks. "Ray explained that he wanted all the songs to tie together, subject-wise, so we knew that much," says Mick Avory. "Ray always kept everything to himself, everything was a big secret," says Pete Quaife. "But when the numbers started to come together, we began to see what he was driving at. About the time of 'Animal Farm', it all clicked."

Meanwhile, Reprise, the group's record label in America, was demanding a new Kinks LP. Under duress, Davies acquiesced. In June 1968, he submitted a fifteen-track ragbag of Village Green songs, singles and off cuts to Reprise, who gave it the provisional title *Four More Respected Gentlemen*, a weak reference to an earlier American Kinks hit. At this stage, Davies seems to have assumed America would not want the finished Village Green album, perhaps judging it too parochial for that market.

By accident or design, Davies' compilation of *Four More Respected Gentlemen* is not quite as random as it first appears. Musically, it contains a high percentage of rockers and fast songs, something emphasised by Reprise's edit of the LP.[4] Moreover, many of Davies' lyrics reflect his uneasy personal and professional situation at the time, being largely concerned with ways of escape: running away ('Polly'), booze ('Misty Water'), cheap music ('Mr. Songbird'), nostalgia ('Picture Book'), one-night stands ('Berkeley Mews'), even suicide ('Did

---

[4]Davies' original tracklisting of *Four More Respected Gentlemen* consisted of 'She's Got Everything', 'Monica', 'Mr. Songbird', 'Johnny Thunder', 'Polly', 'Days', 'Animal Farm', 'Berkeley Mews', 'Picture Book', 'Phenomenal Cat', 'Misty Water', 'Did You See His Name', 'Autumn Almanac' and two Dave Davies numbers, 'Susannah's Still Alive' and 'There Is No Life Without Love'. Reprise removed the last four titles, leaving *FMRG* as a slim eleven-track LP.

You See His Name'). In the event, there were sufficient delays to *Four More Respected Gentlemen* to ensure it was never issued, although acetate copies do exist. Instead, *TKATVGPS* was released in America in January 1969, where contrary to group expectations, it turned out to be the beginning of The Kinks' revival, its Anglo-parochialism the very thing some American listeners liked about it (Gor, darn it).

Meanwhile, tensions in the group had reached a head in May during the recording of 'Days'. Unlike 'Wonderboy', Davies always intended this new song, a bittersweet adieu to a former lover, to be a new Kinks single. Once again, he had something to prove. However, there was a major row in the studio between Davies and Quaife, with the latter storming out. The fight was sparked off by Quaife doodling the word 'Daze' on the box of the 'Days' master tape, a story corroborated by Dave Davies in his autobiography *Kink*. Ray Davies was incensed at Quaife's apparent disregard for his work and his feelings; 'Days' was "the most significant song in my life so far." A screaming match ensued, although Davies concedes it was conceit on his part. "My work had become too precious to me," he wrote in *X-Ray*. "I was literally in an emotional daze about where I was, who I was and who I wanted to be with. Maybe Quaife was as well."[xxxvii] This story has passed into Kinks legend, largely thanks to its retelling in Ray Davies' *Storyteller*

presentations where, as in *X-Ray*, it takes on a retrospective symbolic resonance: "I was convinced Quaife had
decided to leave the band forever . . . 'Days' was telling
the world that it was the end of the group."[xxxviii]

Not surprisingly, Quaife's version of events is slightly
different. In an interview with Bill Orton and Russell
Smith in 1999, he recalled what happened.

> Pete Quaife: "After a while it became colossally bor-
> ing, to sit there listening to this thing over and over
> and over again, so what I was doing was doodling. I
> was drawing this little man and Ray saw it and got
> really upset! I was doodling instead of listening to the
> damn music, and he started making a big fuss about
> it. I went, 'Fuck it Ray, I'm out of here', and I just
> walked out. Rasa came running after me; 'Don't go,
> don't be like that!' I said to hell with it, I'm not going
> to be spoken to like that . . . I was drawing a little
> cartoon character, me. I can even tell you where it
> was on the box . . . for some reason he has changed
> that around to [me] writing the word 'Daze'."
> Russell Smith: "Was that an excuse on Ray's part?"
> PQ: "He thought it makes a better story if he said
> that."[xxxix]

Whatever the exact truth of it, the ill will hung
around as The Kinks embarked on their next misguided
venture, a hastily arranged June tour of Sweden. "We
were staying slightly away from each other," says Quaife.
"It was the best thing to do at that time." To make

matters worse, The Kinks' new agent Barry Dickens had booked the group to play in the open air at a series of Swedish 'folk parks', family leisure parks sponsored by the state. The Kinks had been told they were flying out to play rock festivals; they were taken aback to discover "parents strolling around with kids licking ice-lollies alongside genuine fans and party revellers," recalls Dave Davies in *Kink*. "It was a horrible, soulless experience."[xl] But things would get worse before the year was out.

'Days' was released at the end of June. The single slowly sold a respectable 82,000 copies and hung around the top twenty for several weeks, but reviews were luke-warm. "The brothers Davies sing through another non-descript tune against a barrage of strings — or electronics — it's hard to tell these days," noted *Melody Maker*.[xli] Penny Valentine in *Disc* liked the single ("better than they've done for ages") but in *Melody Maker*'s Blind Date column, Keith Moon of The Who pronounced 'Days' "pretty dated, like one of the songs Pete [Towns-hend] keeps under his sink." He spoke for many. "I dig what The Kinks do, but I've never thought of them as a group."[xlii]

Back from Sweden, The Kinks undertook a final burst of recording for the Village Green album — it is believed 'Wicked Annabella', 'Starstruck', 'People Take Pictures Of Each Other' and the poignant 'Do You

Remember Walter' were all recorded in July 1968. Crucially, Davies made the conceptual leap from Village Green to *TKATVGPS*, writing 'The Village Green Preservation Society', a song he called the album's "national anthem". Some songs still seemed like remnants of a wholly different, personal Ray Davies project. Everything was becoming blurred.

On their return from Sweden, there is some evidence to suggest that, after the disappointments and infighting of the previous months, a ceasefire was brokered. Davies acceded to the band members' requests for more creative input, albeit somewhat reluctantly. "I'm happy the way the recordings are coming out," he said at the time. "I'm getting over to the group more. We're doing what I think the group wants, although it's hard, sometimes, to feel the same way."[xliii] Davies also accepted this album would be The Kinks' new LP.

"We developed it together, which was the first time that had happened really," says Mick Avory. "Because it had a theme, I think he wanted some kind of continuity of feel for it. We were adhesive and locked into each other's ways. He trusted us a bit more."

Pete Quaife looks back on this respite as The Kinks' Indian summer. "I'm not quite sure what it was — either Ray was not feeling too well or he was very tired, maybe it was the court case — but all of us managed to get in ideas and put them over and do them, which was amazing. During rehearsal *and* recording. Just for that little period, he lightened up a lot. In the studio, it was a lot easier to get ideas across or to suggest things." Of course, this may just have been a ruse on Davies' part to get the LP finished. "Towards the end — Boom! He went back to being Ray Davies and that was it. We all went back to living in a haze of 'What the hell is going on?' "

As Davies' creative energies focussed on the end product, the 'preservation' umbrella also permitted him to incorporate some of the more personal songs The Kinks had been working on. "It was a vague idea in the beginning," confirms Pete Quaife, "but then it began to take form as we were recording. Eventually he realised — jeez, I can put this together as *that*."

With the album nearing completion, a release date was pencilled in for late September. In early July, The Kinks recut 'Monica' in two separate radio sessions for the BBC, while at the end of the month, the group appeared on the *Colour Me Pop* strand of BBC 2's *Late Night Line-Up*, performing a selection of numbers that included 'Days', 'Sitting By The Riverside' and 'Picture Book'. In interviews, group members began to puff their forthcoming LP. Dave Davies, who was supposed to be promoting 'Lincoln County', seemed much more excited about *Village Green*, as he referred to it, than his much-delayed third solo single. "It was originally Ray's idea to do it as a stage musical," he told *Disc*.

"That never came off though, so we did it on an LP. It's about a town and the people that have lived there, and the village green is the focal point of the whole thing."[xliv] In *New Musical Express*, he was more effusive. "It's the best thing we've ever done . . . All Ray's songs came at the right time for us, just when we were wondering what to do next."[xlv]

Ray Davies spoke cautiously of the tracks on the album. "They're all related in a way. I hope they will be self-explanatory if people are interested enough to listen. Sometimes I wonder if they really do listen to records."[xlvi] Elsewhere, he revealed he had ditched his solo plans and reaffirmed his commitment to The Kinks. "I've asked the group to sing and play on it with me and they have kindly consented," he told Keith Altham. "I would like to make it clear that I've always wanted to do an LP with the Kinks anyway!"[xlvii]

For the cover of the new album, a photo session was organised on Hampstead Heath. On a balmy August day, the group strolled from Kenwood House out onto the Heath itself, ambling through the long grass with two photographers, Pye's in-house snapper and *Melody Maker*'s Barrie Wentzell. "I'd met The Kinks a few times before and was always a bit scared of them," remembers Wentzell. "To my surprise the boys were dressed casually and seemed in mellower mood. After tea on the terrace we set off across the Heath to take some pictures in the long grass which Hampstead Council used to leave uncut, thus giving the place a truly country feel." One of Wentzell's photographs was used on the rear of the album, although he did not receive a credit (or payment).

"That was one of those days when everyone got on great," says Pete Quaife. "It was long but it was very pleasant. I could take you there now and take you where we walked. Down by the lake, over the bridge . . . " Mick Avory also has fond memories of the day. "We just turned up in what we were wearing. It was nice because it was just down the road from where we lived." Ray Davies looks back on the photo session as The Kinks' last golden day. "When Barry Wentzel (sic.) took those last cover shots outside Kenwood House in Hampstead, he was documenting the end of the band."[xlviii]

In August, Ray Davies left Fortis Green for Borehamwood and The Kinks recorded 'The Village Green Preservation Society'. In theory, the album was now complete. "It's something I wanted to do two years ago," Davies said. "I've got the feeling it is going to work the way I want it to. It will be what I've always wanted. It's just a matter of the things that are on it."[xlix] The unhappy significance of this last comment would only become apparent in the weeks ahead.

Davies initially sequenced a twelve-track version of *TKATVGPS*, which was glowingly previewed by Keith Altham in *NME* on September 21st, singling out the title track for special praise. "This is Mr. D's personal musical museum," he wrote of the album as a whole. "It's worth more than just a thought." Pye advertisements appeared in the pop papers showing a black and white cover design (reproduced in the booklet of the current British edition of the album).[5]

"I went up to their managers' office to listen to a tape," recalls Altham. "It was very interesting from a musical and aesthetic point of view, and I liked it, but I knew it was a Ray Davies solo album in all but name. There was something missing in terms of dynamics. It was an interesting cameo of English class structure, but it didn't seem to have that anger, the kind of attack that Dave used to bring. For The Kinks, I thought it was risky. Ray had this way of writing that, within itself, was ambiguous. And although the album was clever, it didn't seem to me to have the ambiguity that his best

---

[5]The original tracklisting is as follows. 'The Village Green Preservation Society', 'Do You Remember Walter', 'Picture Book', 'Johnny Thunder', 'Monica', 'Days', 'Village Green', 'Mr. Songbird', 'Wicked Annabella', 'Starstruck', 'Phenomenal Cat', 'People Take Pictures Of Each Other'.

work had — or maybe it had too much. Either way, it was a bit too twee."

TKATVGPS was scheduled to appear in the shops on September 27th 1968, a week after Altham's preview. It never made it. At the very last minute, Ray Davies had a change of heart.[6] He wanted the album postponed. More, he wanted to expand it to a double album, and went to Pye with the suggestion that the album could be sold at a budget price, twenty new Kinks tracks in one fell swoop.[7] Pye refused but a compromise was reached — Davies could resequence a fifteen-track edition of the album as a single disc. He agreed, but rather than draw on The Kinks' considerable backlog of material, he took the group back into the studio in October to record two new songs — the awe-inspiring 'Big Sky' and a gently satirical number called 'Last Of The Steam-Powered Trains'.

There has been much debate as to why Davies took the drastic action of pulling the original LP. An explanation has never been forthcoming and we can only sur-

---

[6]Davies' decision was taken so late in the day that Pye had already shipped production tapes to some of its foreign subsidiaries, and the album was released in its twelve-track incarnation in France, Italy, Sweden / Norway, and New Zealand, all of whom produced unique, and now very collectable, artwork.
[7]This tracklisting is not known, and it is uncertain it was ever finalised.

mise. *TKATVGPS* was the album he had been working on for two years. Davies was a perfectionist, and by this stage his perfectionism was verging on the neurotic, indulged by a management and record company who hoped The Kinks' main man would soon recapture his hit making form. In a sense, he was also reluctant to finish the project, describing it as "a pet dream". The album was already highly personal; now it represented the missed opportunity of a solo career as well, a decisive break from the grind of 'the hit machine'. He may have been aware that both The Beatles and The Jimi Hendrix Experience were preparing to release double albums. He may have felt that too much fine material would end up in a vault somewhere, which as it transpired, is mostly what happened. But above all, one suspects Ray Davies knew this was his best work — he was desperate to get it right.

Meanwhile, The Kinks' professional standing sank lower and lower, as did their finances. In October, they were forced to accept cabaret residences at northern working mens' clubs like the Fiesta Club, Stockton-on-Tees, and The Top Hat, Spennymoor. The shows were a disaster. Dave Davies would down a whole bottle of Scotch before going on stage. "You had to have a set that was slick, polished and rehearsed, and that's what we weren't," says Mick Avory. "We were so out of our depth," laments Pete Quaife. "It was kind of difficult to imagine middle-aged men screaming. They'd stare at us, then as soon as we finished they'd order another round of beer and get on with talking about what had happened down at t'mine! But we had to do it because we didn't have any other work."

The Kinks limped on. On November 22nd, the album Ray Davies had spent two years writing and recording, refining and perfecting, was finally released. Yet, to anyone who actually bought it that Friday, an air of haste or neglect was immediately apparent — there were discrepancies between the song titles on the label and cover (three on side one alone) and even a misprint: 'Phenominal (sic.) Cat'. Pye placed a few more small advertisements in the pop papers and Davies discussed the different tracks in *Melody Maker*. The LP received just one notice, a positive write-up in *Disc*, whose nameless reviewer remarked that Davies had managed to by-pass "everything psychedelic and electronic", and concluded: "The Kinks may not be on the crest of the pop wave these days, but Ray Davies will remain one of our finest composers for many years."[1] It was too little, too late. Davies' last-minute reworkings had fatally undermined any momentum the album may have had in September, and Pye was simply not equipped to market the LP in the way companies like Apple or Track could. People bought one another 'The White Album' or *Electric Ladyland* or the Rolling Stones' newie *Beggars Banquet* for Christmas in 1968 and forgot about *TKATVGPS*, if they even knew it existed in the first place. In an age of street-fighting men and revolution, the hit faces of 1966 singing songs about village greens, cricket and trips to the seaside sounded middle-aged, reactionary and suicidally unhip. It seemed The Kinks were over.

"You could see everything was winding down," says Pete Quaife. "It wasn't a madcap, hit-a-week type of affair any more. It was becoming more like *work*, y'know?" Quaife would leave in March 1969, after contributing to the never-released Dave Davies solo LP and the rotten 'Plastic Man', and The Kinks would become a different group, in more ways than one.

However, posterity would vindicate Ray Davies. The fifteen-track *TKATVGPS* is a work of art. By adding the two new songs and two earlier tracks ('Sitting By The Riverside' and 'All Of My Friends Were There') and dropping 'Days' and 'Mr. Songbird', he created an album whose songs seem to talk to each other, and whose intelligence, sense of humour and humanity echo down the decades, whatever its author may feel about it today.

It will be soon be forty years since *TKATVGPS* was released. Enthusiasm for the 1960's swings on unabated, but the sensibility of the album is a modern one. While many of its lyrics deal with the sweet scent of the past, and the LP owes at least some of its longevity to a collective nostalgia — for The Kinks or the near-mythical 60's — the album's fifteen songs ring with insight and self-awareness. It is emphatically not a period piece. The Kinks aren't The Village Green Preservation Society; there is more to it than that. The proof lays equally in the well-worn grooves of a much-loved LP or the data stream of a new CD or downloaded audio file. Listen . . .

Chapter Two —
The Kinks Are
The Village Green
Preservation Society

The English village green is a little patch of grassland
that still strikes a chord in the hearts of most native
men and women two hundred years after the Indus-
trial Revolution changed the majority of us to urban
dwellers. It represents rural peace and quiet, as well
as a community spirit that does not obtain in towns,
and sets up in most of us a yearning for that fondly
imagined country paradise, lost by the growth of im-
perialism and capitalism which have made England
an over-populated country of noisy and dirty towns
and cities where the mass of men, as Thoreau put it,
lead lives of quiet desperation.

    The English Village Green, Brian Bailey, 1985

The Village Green
Preservation Society

By the summer of 1968, Ray Davies was still without a title for the forthcoming Kinks album. *Village Green*, the project's working title, seemed too narrow — the original Village Green concept had mutated as other, more personal songs joined the fray and, although the track 'Village Green' remained essential to Davies' plan for the album, it would be two years old by the time the LP was released. Things had moved on.

"I was looking for a title for the album about three months ago, when we had finished most of the tracks," Davies told *Saturday Club*'s Brian Matthew in November, a few days before the record finally reached the shops, "and somebody said that one of the things The Kinks have been doing for the last three years is preserving."[li] The suggestion was clearly enough to prompt Davies towards not just a title for his album, but also to compose what he subsequently described as its "national anthem" — 'The Village Green Preservation Society.' "This started out to be a solo album for me," he told Bob Dawbarn in *Melody Maker*, "but somebody mentioned to me that The Kinks do try to preserve things — we are all for that looking back thing. I thought it would be a nice idea to try and sum it up in one song."[lii]

At first glance, the basic elements of 'The Village Green Preservation Society' seem to betray the speed with which it was manufactured — four strummed chords with a simple, circling melody, modulating from C major to D major at 1:12. However, its structure is unorthodox and unpredictable, the arrangement is pin-sharp and the performances are self-assured. And then there is Davies' deceptively acerbic lyric, which could so easily have been a showcase for resourceful use of the thesaurus (consortium, affinity, affiliate, er, vernacular . . .) and not much besides, but which transcends its own ingenuity to stand alongside its author's finest moments — heartfelt, whimsical, and recklessly unfashionable.

'The Village Green Preservation Society' is carefully set up as a slow burn, everything leading to Davies' seemingly off-the-cuff "God save the village green!" as the track begins to fade. Much of the credit for the success of this arrangement must go to Mick Avory, whose drumming is especially exuberant. The opening piano figure is similarly light and effortless.[8] Ray's close harmony vocal with Dave Davies is sustained throughout, dropping away for Ray to emphasise the last line before the modulation to D. Only at the song's close

---

[8]This may or may not be Nicky Hopkins. The slightly slower BBC version recorded on 26/11/68 (and available on *BBC Sessions 1964–1977*), on which the piano part is definitely played by Davies, reveals a somewhat less steady hand on the keyboard.

does Davies purposefully move centre stage (literally, if you are listening in stereo), singing the last two lines solo with a backwash of falsetto harmonies. "God save the village green!" We're left in no doubt as to whose Preservation Society, and whose album, this is.

"All the things in the song are things are things I'd like to see preserved," said Davies at the time.[liii] "I like village greens and preservation societies," he told Jonathan Cott. "I like Donald Duck, Desperate Dan, draught beer."[liv] This is disingenuous and, as Davies belatedly realised, open to misinterpretation. "A lot of people accuse me in the song of being kind of fascist," he has said. "Traditional, you know? But it's not. It's a warm feeling, like a fantasy world that I can retreat to."[lv] As noted by Robert Christgau in his influential appraisal of the album in *Village Voice*, "Does Davies really want to preserve virginity? Presumably not. But the fictional form allows him to remain ambivalent."[lvi]

However, there is a satirical edge to 'The Village Green Preservation Society' that has been dulled or lost in the years since its release.

1968 was not a comfortable year for Britain and the British. The anti-Vietnam protests outside the American embassy in Grosvenor Square were the most violent manifestation of a general post-colonial unease with Britain's diminishing role in the world. The economic climate was deteriorating, causing the Labour government to launch its "I'm Backing Britain" initiative as a spur to the consumer to buy British-made goods and support British industry in the wake of devaluation of the pound. The entertainer Bruce Forsyth released a single on Pye, called 'I'm Backing Britain', co-written by Pye's musical director Tony Hatch ("Let's keep it going / The good times are blowing our way").

1968 was also the year Conservative MP Enoch Powell urged the repatriation of African and West Indian immigrants in a speech which quickly passed into infamy: "As I look ahead I am filled with foreboding. Like the Roman, I seem to see the River Tiber foaming with blood." People marched against Powell, and for him. In a photograph from the time, an Asian woman balances her baby in one hand and a homemade placard in the other: 'WE ARE BACKING BRITAIN'. Meanwhile a group of porters from Smithfield meat market demonstrate in their blood-spattered overalls, laughing and carrying a banner: 'SMITHFIELD SAYS: A GEORGE CROSS FOR ENOCH'.

So 1968 was a year of anger and unrest, of fear of the future and nostalgia for a safer past, of preservation societies, affinities and affiliates, not all of them wholesome — something Davies was undoubtedly aware of. Early in the year, he had penned a satirical song called

'We're Backing Britain' for the BBC TV programme *At the Eleventh Hour*.[9] In this context, the lyrics of 'The Village Green Preservation Society' are less quaint, less escapist; rather, they mock the certainties of protest

---

[9]Davies wrote at least nine songs for *At The Eleventh Hour*, a late night satire programme in the mould of *That Was The Week That Was*. As noted by Doug Hinman, they were performed in the show by jazz singer Jeannie Lamb with light orchestral backing, and included 'You Can't Give More Than What You Have', 'If Christmas Day Could Last Forever', 'We're Backing Britain', 'Could Be You're Getting Old', 'This Is What The World Is All About', 'The Man Who Conned Dinner From the Ritz', 'Did You See His Name', 'Poor Old Intellectual Sadie' and 'Just A Poor Country Girl'. None were recorded by the Kinks, with the exception of 'Did You See His Name', which was cut during *TKATVGPS* sessions in May 1968 and finally released four years later on the Reprise compilation *The Kink Kronikles*. The following year, Davies repeated the stunt, writing five songs for the television series *Where Was Spring?* These were recorded by The Kinks, but only two have so far surfaced officially — 'Where Did My Spring Go?' and 'When I Turn Off The Living Room Light', both on *The Great Lost Kinks Album*. The remaining three — 'Darling I Respect You', 'Let's Take Off All Our Clothes' and (probably) 'We Are Two Of A Kind' are still missing, though a near-unlistenable off-air copy of the first of these is circulating on bootleg. In May 1971, it was announced in the music papers that an album containing some or all these songs — *Songs I Sang For Auntie / The Ray Davies Songbook* — was underway for release later that same year. Of course, it never appeared. Neither the BBC, nor Sanctuary, nor Reprise hold copies of the missing songs, either in complete or demo form. We can only hope that, somewhere deep in the bowels of Konk Studios, Raymond Douglas Davies is keeping them safe.

with a list of utterly idiosyncratic demands, then make a personal plea for moderation: what more can we do? "I'm not particularly patriotic — perhaps I'm just selfish," Davies told Derek Boltwood six months after the album was released, "but I like these traditional British things to be there. I never go to watch cricket any more, but I like to know it's there. . . . It all sounds terribly serious, but it isn't really — I mean, I wouldn't die for this cause, but I think it's frightfully important."[lvii]

It may lack the righteousness and glamour of 'Street Fighting Man', but unlike The Rolling Stones' modish call to arms, Davies' quiet song of defiance is not a pose. Taken either as autobiography or satire, as a curtain raiser for the album, or as the world's gentlest and most oblique protest song, 'The Village Green Preservation Society' is central to Davies' map of the Village Green, and the great theme of his songwriting at this time — the ambiguous allure of the past. The Kinks simply dusted it with magic and passed it on.

Do You Remember Walter

"The past is a curious thing," says George Bowling, the middle-aged narrator of George Orwell's *Coming Up For Air*. "It's with you all the time."[lviii] Bowling, a dissatisfied insurance salesman, fat and washed up in a stagnating marriage, yearns for the landscape of his childhood.

"What was it that people had in those days?" he wonders. "A feeling of security, even when they weren't secure. More exactly, it was a feeling of continuity."[lix] These could be the words of Ray Davies in 1968, contemplating a bygone age and all of twenty-four years old.

In *Coming Up For Air*, George Bowling contrives an escape from the routine and frustration of his day-to-day existence by returning to Lower Binfield, the small country town in which he grew up. The trip is a disaster. Lower Binfield has changed almost beyond recognition; Bowling's long wished-for homecoming brings only disillusionment and despair, depriving him even of the safe haven of his memories. There is no return because, of course, there cannot be. Elsie, the sweetheart Bowling left behind twenty-five years earlier, is now married to a tobacconist. She is old at forty-seven, her hair completely grey. More to the point, "She didn't know me from Adam. I was just a customer, a stranger, an uninteresting fat man . . . she didn't even recognise me. If I told her who I was, very likely she wouldn't remember."[lx]

If the title track is the national anthem of *TKATVGPS*, 'Do You Remember Walter' is its lyrical heart. It is one of Davies' finest songs, a meditation on friendship and time which, in common with his best work, takes an everyday image or commonplace event (commuters at Waterloo, the stars on Hollywood Boulevard) and finds the universe within it. "Walter was a friend of mine, we used to play football together every Saturday," said Davies shortly before the album's release. "Then I met him again after about five years and we found out we didn't have anything to talk about."[lxi] Davies transformed this awkwardness into art.

Five years, says Davies, yet Walter reminds him of "a world I knew *so long ago*", a world before the Kinks, before the hits, the screaming and the breakdowns — hardly surprising there wasn't much to say, especially if the famous pop star only wanted to linger on the old times. They were going to be free, Ray and Walter; like Edward Lear's Owl and Pussycat, they were going to sail away to sea ("in a beautiful pea-green boat / They took some honey / And plenty of money . . . ") but somehow they never did it. And yet, Davies seems to suggest, in the end neither man would wish for the other's fate — Walter is bored by the singer's reminiscing, while Davies scoffs at Walter's early bedtime (and conformity). In the final reckoning, that isn't what counts. "There's a line in the lyric — 'People often change but memories of people remain' (sic.) — which sums up what this is about," said Davies,[lxii] and at the song's conclusion he slows everything down to emphasise the point. The awkwardness, the sadness of things, Davies says, is the price we pay for change, but we should try to preserve the memory regardless.

ANDY MILLER

Davies matched the winding, conversational lyric of 'Do You Remember Walter' with one of his most precocious melodies. The tune skips up and down the scale like a piano exercise (see also: 'Picture Book', 'People Take Pictures Of Each Other'). That the finished track sounds neither precious nor pretentious is a tribute to Davies' single-minded arrangement — every instrument and production nuance has been made a slave to the lyric and the vocal. Against the measured pounding of the piano and bass (and Mick Avory's Boys' Brigade snare rolls), Davies sings with passionate restraint, his vocal track cleverly enhanced by some occasional double-tracking and a hazy Mellotron line that shadows the melody; like Walter, an echo. The effect is rousing at times, melancholic at others. Having paused to deliver the song's parting shot, the Mellotron line is left behind as the track fades, as if to bear it out — our memories are what remains long after names have been forgotten.[10]

---

[10]As was the custom of the day, there are clear differences between the mono and stereo mixes of some *TKATVGPS* tracks, and indeed between a handful of numbers on the twelve and fifteen track editions. At this stage, mono was still Ray Davies' preferred format. In the case of 'Do You Remember Walter', the differences are minor: a little more of Dave's guitar, a little less Mellotron, and no tambourine. Both mixes are included on the current British edition of the album.

Picture Book

In 2002, Ray Davies was called upon to pen sleeve notes for his own various artists tribute album, *This Is Where I Belong: The Songs Of Ray Davies & The Kinks*. There are three selections from *TKATVGPS* on the album, of which 'Picture Book' is one; "brave" is how Davies describes Bill Lloyd and Tommy Womack's decision to tackle it. The song was not written for The Kinks. "They were songs that I should have consigned to my private collection," he writes. "Both songs ['Picture Book' and 'Muswell Hillbilly'] are inspired by my family and mention people that really existed."[lxiii]

Yet, from the beginning, 'Picture Book' was always one of *TKATVGPS*'s most visible and significant songs. Recorded in the spring of 1968, it was selected by Davies for the aborted *Four More Respected Gentlemen*, and for both twelve and fifteen-track versions of the album where, as noted above, it falls in behind 'The Village Green Preservation Society' and 'Do You Remember Walter', the opening triumvirate that introduces the major themes and images of the LP. The Kinks also included 'Picture Book' in their July 26th appearance on the *Colour Me Pop* strand of BBC 2's *Late Night Line-Up*, a full five months ahead of the album's release. The group performed it again the following February on another BBC 2 music programme *Once More With Felix*, hosted by the folk singer Julie Felix.[11]

In other words, however Ray Davies may feel about it today, 'Picture Book' was an important song to The Kinks and an important piece of the whole Village Green jigsaw. In the studio, Pete Quaife recalls being drilled through multiple takes of the track, as Davies struggled to get it finished to his satisfaction. 'Picture Book' is a scruffier proposition than either of the songs that precede it, the final minute a mish-mash of assorted "yeah yeah yeah"s, "na na na"s, and even a "scooby dooby doo" or two, lifted from Sinatra's 'Strangers In The Night', and crooned by Davies in suitably ironic fashion. Despite their reported fatigue, The Kinks' play-

---

[11]Both these shows are missing from the BBC archives, presumed wiped. *Colour Me Pop* is the greater loss. The Kinks wore their colourful late Sixties stage outfits and performed some or all of 'Dedicated Follower Of Fashion', 'A Well Respected Man', 'Death Of A Clown', 'Sunny Afternoon', 'Lincoln County', 'Picture Book', 'Sitting By The Riverside', 'She's Got Everything' (filmed insert), 'Two Sisters' and 'Days'. It is not known if this was a live or lip-synched performance, but note the inclusion of two tracks from *TKATVGPS* so far in advance of the album's release. It seems likely that these renditions varied from what appeared on the finished LP. The other song performed on *Once More With Felix* (recorded 8th January 1969, broadcast 1st February) was 'Last Of The Steam-Powered Trains'.

ing sounds enthusiastic. The track progresses so jauntily, in fact, that one can easily miss the grit at its centre; these family photographs were taken "a long time ago" and the happiness they represent — the happiness of childhood — has gone forever.

"No one could afford a bloody camera," Dave Davies told Bill Orton in 2001. "I didn't know anybody that had a camera, not even on our street. It wasn't a big thing, unless you went on holiday — Ramsgate or whatever. We had pictures of that . . . "[lxiv] Two such pictures are reproduced in Dave's autobiography. In one, Ray Davies, no more than twelve years old, stands on the beach between his brother Dave and their nephew Terry (the son of their sister Rosie and her husband Arthur, both of whom would one day have songs, whole albums, written about them). Dave and Terry are on all fours, like dogs; Ray is holding them both by the hair, grinning from ear to ear.

The other snap is of Gwen and Rene, two more Davies sisters. Dave thinks the photos date from around June 1957. Within weeks, Ray would turn thirteen. For his birthday Rene would buy him a Spanish guitar. Then, against doctor's orders, she would go out dancing to the Lyceum Ballroom in the Strand, where she would collapse on the dance floor. She died that night. "What dreadful mixed feelings my brother must have experienced on that following morning," writes Dave Davies. "For months he had been on and on about that bloody guitar . . ."[lxv]

So the gaiety of 'Picture Book' — "a paper hat, kiss-me-quick" song as Ray described it — masks an even greater sense of personal loss than that portrayed in 'Do You Remember Walter'. To Ray Davies, the photographs are reminders both of happier times and of time lost, an ambivalence more fully expressed in 'People Take Pictures Of Each Other' (on *This Is Where I Belong*, Bill Lloyd and Tommy Womack's "brave" cover version of 'Picture Book' concludes with a snatch of the latter song). Also recorded by The Kinks at this time was the marvellous 'Pictures In The Sand', released only briefly on *The Great Lost Kinks Album*. The song shares 'Picture Book"s seaside setting and end-of-the-pier musical jollity, and also its quiet desperation; although these pictures aren't permanent like photographs, they still can't picture love, in the here and now, vanished or taken away.

*   *   *

The opening trio of tracks on *TKATVGPS* had no equivalent in the pop scene of 1968, chart or underground, in either sound or subject. This wasn't merely unfashionable; it was anathema to the prevailing rock culture of the time, one that embraced Concepts but struggled with ideas. In a year when musicianship for its own sake was on the rise and "feel" was all, when people could conceive of nothing finer than to boogie with Canned Heat, Davies makes it plain that everything on *TKATVGPS* — arrangement, performance, production — will be the servant of the song, and the songs will be about ordinary things and everyday people: "I go out of my way to like ordinary things. I cling on to the simple values . . . I think 'ordinary' people are quite complex enough without looking for greater sophistication . . . We do a lot of stompy things. The rhythms are reminiscent of the Twenties. I like the old days. Everybody does — in song."[lxvi] Ignoring what was happening around him, Ray Davies pursued his particular vision to its conclusion and in doing so consigned the LP to swift obscurity and broke The Kinks.

But what more could he do?

Johnny Thunder

Another track selected for *Four More Respected Gentlemen* and both incarnations of *TKATVGPS*, 'Johnny Thunder' neatly fits Davies' original "town and the people who live there" conception of *Village Green*, as LP, stage musical or whatever. "It's about a rocker," he said. "I wrote it after Wild One (sic.) was released."[lxvii] László

Benedek's 1954 film *The Wild One*, starring Marlon Brando and Lee Marvin as the leaders of rival biker gangs, had been reissued to London cinemas in early 1968. Brando's character is called Johnny, and it may be Brando that Davies had in mind as his model for Johnny Thunder (try swapping the names around the next time you're singing along).[12] "He's the local hound — a real swine," Dave told *Disc and Music Echo*, before reassuring readers "but he's inside at the moment!"[lxviii]

'Johnny Thunder' is one of the more straightforward songs on *TKATVGPS*, with few production tricks and a rare solo vocal from Ray, his first on the album not to be double-tracked at any point. Acoustic guitars, bass and drums are joined by Dave Davies' treated and tidy guitar part, mixed almost out of earshot — a shame, as the countermelody that accompanies the chorus and "thunder and lightning" refrain is delightful. The brass band-like wordless vocal line provides a melodic flourish, while once again the rhythm section has been given some space to stretch out and The Kinks' harmonies are characteristically imaginative (if a little ragged).

---

[12]Rock historians please note: the rival gangs of *The Wild One* have now supplied two bands with names — The Beetles have been joined by the Black Rebel Motorcycle Club.

Davies' portrait of the rebel motorcyclist who rides alone, subsisting on nothing but the elements, is so idealized as to be untrustworthy (an unreliable narrator is another literary aspect of the songs on *TKATVGPS*, notably 'Village Green' itself). The inhabitants may not be able to reach Johnny, but he is a much-loved feature of the town nevertheless — he is even in Helena's prayers. Johnny, like Walter, has sworn to be free, and in the process has been turned into a perfectly preserved — and thus neutered — icon of rebellion, just as pictures of Marlon Brando in *The Wild One* eventually decorated a million bedroom walls. God bless him indeed (and tudor houses, china cups, virginity etc.). The character, fleshed out somewhat, reappears as 'One Of The Survivors' on *Preservation Act 1*.

According to Dave Davies, the original 'Johnny Thunder' attracted the attention of a longstanding Kinks' admirer: Pete Townshend of The Who. Davies alleges Townshend so liked the song's dramatic opening riff that he quickly recycled it in his own work — after all, The Who's guitarist had form where The Kinks were concerned. He openly admitted to modelling 'I Can't Explain' on The Kinks' first few hits, and Dave suspected Ray and Pete's mutual friend Barry Fantoni of "conveying our ideas to Townshend". Dave declines to say exactly where this new "tribute" occurred, but listeners to *Tommy*, released just six months after *TKATVGPS*, may detect some similarity between 'Johnny Thunder' and parts of 'Overture' and 'Go To The Mirror!'

Ray may have agreed with his brother. Speaking to *Rolling Stone* in November 1969, by which time *Tommy*, rock's much-hyped first opera, had become a sensation and turned Townshend and his group into superstars, Davies had this to say on the subject of 'Johnny Thunder'. "It's not a cowboy song," he told Jonathan Cott, pleasantly. "It would be nice to hear The Who sing it."[lxix]

Last Of The Steam-Powered Trains

From thunder and lightning to 'Smokestack Lightnin''. 'Last Of The Steam-Powered Trains' was a very late addition to *TKATVGPS* and evidence suggests it was probably the last song to be composed for the album. Like 'Big Sky', it was recorded in October 1968, after the cancellation of the original twelve-track edition. In several respects, the song is uncharacteristic of the album as a whole — its R&B derivation, its live-sounding performance and its four-minute length are all atypical[13]

---

[13]No other song on *TKATVGPS* exceeds three minutes, let alone four.

— but in another it is the quintessence of Davies' writing for this project. On a LP full of deceptively acidic songs, 'Last Of The Steam-Powered Trains' may well be the most corrosive of them all.

The Kinks, in common with many of the pop era's finest groups, emerged from the Rhythm and Blues boom of the early sixties. Among the most totemic R&B favourites was a sinister, sensual half-shuffle called 'Smokestack Lightnin'' by Chester Burnett a.k.a. The Howlin' Wolf. By 1963, the song was a staple of every self-respecting British R&B band's act. The High Numbers performed 'Smokestack Lightnin'' at their unsuccessful Abbey Road audition in October 1964. In Southampton, there was even a group called The Howlin' Wolves (later to change their name and find brief fame as reluctant psychedelic nabobs Simon Dupree and the Big Sound).

It may be nearly fifty years old, but the original 'Smokestack Lightnin'' is a jawdropping record, a despatch from some sweltering, moonlit chamber, sung with the kind of elemental, roaring fervour that only Don Van Vliet, alias Captain Beefheart, has ever seemed able to match. In comparison, recorded British beat boom versions of the song tend to be either long on fretwork and short on menace (The Yardbirds) or well intentioned but hopelessly callow (Manfred Mann).

By late 1963, Howlin' Wolf's original recording of 'Smokestack Lightnin'' was in such demand that Pye issued it as the lead track of a moderately successful EP. Six months later — around the time The Kinks were fighting with the same label to get 'You Really Got Me' rerecorded with more power and atmosphere — the company issued 'Smokestack Lightnin'' again, this time as a single. Howlin' Wolf, six foot three and nearly three hundred pounds, made a memorable appearance as the surprise guest on BBC TV's *Jukebox Jury*, where he towered over the suddenly quaking members of a panel who had just voted his greatest hit a 'Miss'.

By mid-1965 however, the R&B scene was in decline as pop proliferated and groups increasingly came under pressure, often from their own management, to compete with The Beatles and write their own pop-orientated material. Out went the repertoire. In *X-Ray*, Davies recounts Hal Carter's advice to the Kinks about tailoring their stage act: "Cut out that 'Smokestack Lightning' number. You're not doing yourselves and anybody else any favours by playing that."[lxx] Meanwhile, The High Numbers, now with a new name and a record deal, were changing their tune(s). "The Who are having serious doubts about the state of R&B," their manager Kit Lambert told *Disc*. "Now the LP material [for *My Generation*] will consist of hard pop. They've finished with 'Smokestack Lightning'."[lxxi]

So in 1968, by basing 'Last Of The Steam-Powered Trains' on an instantly recognisable riff from four or five years earlier, Ray Davies was blowing the whistle both on himself and his R&B contemporaries. There are jokes and allusions to 'Smokestack Lightnin'', and the scene in general, scattered throughout the song. Like Howlin' Wolf's original track and subsequent covers of it, 'Last Of The Steam-Powered Trains' chugs along in E major. At 2.21, Ray Davies can distantly be heard emitting a scrawny falsetto howl, more afghan hound than wolf. From 3.41 to 3.44, The Kinks double the tempo for two bars, Pete Quaife leaping an octave to play a distinctly Chuck Berry-like bass line. In the third verse there is a lyrical allusion to 'Train Kept A-Rollin'', recorded by The Yardbirds and famously performed by the Jeff Beck / Jimmy Page line-up of the group in Michelangelo Antonioni's *Blow-Up* (1966).[14] And throughout, there is Ray, huffing and puffing away on the harmonica — double-tracked in places: how else do you blow lead and rhythm simultaneously? — like it was 1963 again and The Kinks were back in the pubs and youth clubs of Muswell Hill and East Finchley.

"This was a case of the idea coming before the song," Ray Davies told *Melody Maker* when the album was

---

[14]For copyright reasons, the song was quickly rewritten on the film's set as 'Stroll On'.

released. "Again, like the 'Walter' song it's really about not having anything in common with people. Everybody wanted to know about steam trains a couple of years ago, but they don't any more. It's about me being the last of the renegades. All my friends are middle class now. They've all stopped playing in clubs. They've all made money and have happy faces. Oddly enough I never did like steam trains much."[lxxii]

The correlation of steam trains and R&B in 'Last Of The Steam-Powered Trains' is inspired, both in its witty juxtaposition of such distinctly English and American archetypes, and in the hesitancy it expresses on behalf of its author. Look, Davies says, you, we, loved this music but there is something increasingly ridiculous and misplaced about our love — an English middle class, middle-aged 'Smokestack Lightnin'' is about as authentically bluesy as the Titfield Thunderbolt. I am the last renegade; how absurd that is.

Accordingly, on record the track hovers between paying homage to the R&B sound and spoofing it. Although The Kinks play it straight, some aptly locomotive touches have been added to the arrangement. The group locks into the well-worn groove, picking up speed (and handclaps) as they go. After throwing some ascending chords onto the fire (2.56 to 3.05), they race through the song's final minute, grinding to a halt with a final puff of smoke from Mick Avory's cymbals and kick drum.

It should be too contrived for words; what prevents it from collapsing into novelty is, once again, Davies' lyric, and the despair that runs just beneath its surface jocularity and pride. Like Johnny Thunder, the Last of the Steam-Powered Trains is a rebel, a survivor, who has avoided becoming bourgeois and grey like his friends. Sweat and blood, soot and scum. But such freedom comes at a cost. He is kept in a museum; preservation is driving him mad. By the time he composed the song, Ray Davies had been writing Village Green material for two years, and 'Last Of The Steam-Powered Trains' reiterates its central dilemmas with wit and assurance. How do you reconcile your past and present? How do you stop the weight of experience from dragging you under? How do you keep rollin' when all you want to do is stop?

Reports of the death of British R&B would prove to be greatly exaggerated. In the same month that The Kinks cut 'Last Of The Steam-Powered Trains', thereby bringing to a close the protracted sessions for *TKATVGPS*, south of the river at Olympic Studios in Barnes, Yardbirds guitarist Jimmy Page's new group was recording its debut LP. In a mere thirty-six hours, the irresistible force of Led Zeppelin remade rhythm and blues as hard rock and, in doing so, invented the 1970s. The first song the group ever played together was 'Train Kept A-Rollin''.

'Last Of The Steam-Powered Trains' became a fixture of The Kinks' live act when they returned to America in October 1969; at the Boston Tea Party on the 23rd it was their opening number. Tapes reveal that the record's ironies and nuances have all been ditched in favour of some fully-fledged and unfortunate Zep-like noodling. The song has become the sort of blues workout Davies originally sought to lampoon. By the end of the tour, on the stage of the Fillmore West, San Francisco, it stretches to seven tedious minutes; at the same venue a year later it has swollen to a mind-numbing eleven. Ray bellows the words, jumbling and repeating the lyrics; Dave gives full rein to his incipient guitar heroics. "I was walking in a field one day," yells Dave Davies at one point, bafflingly, "and I happened to look up at the sky. And man, you know what I saw? I SAW AN ALBATROSS!!!" Cue seven minutes of maximum heaviosity (and boredom). It must have sounded great if you were stoned, or one of the musicians, or both.

Coincidentally, Bay Area extemporisers The Grateful Dead regularly featured 'Smokestack Lightnin'' in their interminable concerts. It would be nice to think that The Kinks' "coals to Newcastle" live performances of 'Last Of The Steam-Powered Trains' in San Francisco were extending the song's satirical reach; in fact they were just playing to the long-haired, droopy-lidded gallery. By chance, the song fitted the back-to-rock-basics mood of the times.

One last thought: in its acknowledgement of pop's inevitable greying, 'Last Of The Steam-Powered Trains' has proved to be gloriously predictive. Magazines like *Mojo* and *Classic Rock*, with their emphasis on classicism and authenticity — even iconoclastic movements like punk and techno are now revered for their classicism and authenticity — are like museums of rock music, with figures like Ray Davies and albums like *TKATVGPS* their prize exhibits.

Big Sky

Ray Davies wrote the immortal 'Big Sky' on the balcony of the Carlton Hotel in Cannes. "I spent an evening with all these people doing deals," he said. "The next morning at the Carlton Hotel I watched the sun come up and I looked at them all down there, all going out to do their deals. That's where I got the "Big Sky looking down on all the people" line. It started from there."[lxxiii] In his liner notes for *This Is Where I Belong*, Davies says he watched the sun set, not rise: whatever, the combination of the awe-inspiring skies above the Mediterranean and the businessmen below in their suits and ties was enough to make him consider the existence of "a being somewhat bigger than all of the hustlers around me."[lxxiv] He completed the resulting song quickly, boarded a plane and brought it back to London.[15]

'Big Sky' is not a song about God, but about how human beings cope in a world where God is seemingly unconcerned at their plight. The Big Sky is not dead but preoccupied, benign but indifferent. For Ray Davies, this is a cause for celebration, or at least consolation. The Big Sky is so big, our troubles are small in comparison — and these too shall pass. Freedom comes to everyone in the end, whether we want it or not. Until then, don't let your sorrow get the better of you. The song is a memo both to himself and the Big Sky over his head. It is as good as anything written in the 1960's, by Lennon and McCartney, Bob Dylan or anyone else.

As noted above, 'Big Sky' was recorded in October 1968, just weeks before the final version of the LP reached the shops. As such, it represents the high point of Davies' creativity in the Village Green period and also its final flowering. He would go on to write great songs, and The Kinks would continue to make good records, occasionally great ones, but the rhapsodic,

---

[15]Davies may also have copped the title from Howard Hawks' 1952 movie *The Big Sky*.

sweeping 'Big Sky' is the last in a line of Kinks classics that began with 'Sunny Afternoon' in 1966 and which, because of the fundamental change in the way Davies viewed his writing and career after the failure of *TKATVGPS*, the group never quite regained.

Why did Davies wait nine months before cutting 'Big Sky' with The Kinks? The simple answer may be that this pillar of ... *The Village Green Preservation Society* is not really a Village Green number at all (unless you think the Big Sky is looking down on Johnny Thunder, Walter, Wicked Annabella et al). It shares few of the LP's preoccupations with memory and desire and may, like 'Picture Book', have been intended only for Davies' "private collection"; alternatively, it may have been earmarked for the solo album which, in early 1968, Davies still hoped to make. However, by the autumn, with his solo project a distant memory and Pye rejecting his request for a double album of the songs he and The Kinks had been safeguarding for nearly a year, Davies seems to have realized that if 'Big Sky' were to be heard at all, it would have to be on *TKATVGPS*, and that a new Kinks LP could only benefit from its inclusion. So, at the last minute, The Kinks returned to Pye Studio 2.

A fittingly divine inspiration seems to have visited them there, for the Kinks' version of 'Big Sky' contains some of the most beautiful, thunderous music they ever recorded, aligned to a vulnerability and warmth no other group — and I mean no other group — could ever hope to equal. It is a perfectly balanced production. On the one hand, the mesh of clattering drums and electric guitar never threatens to overwhelm the melody; on the other, the gossamer-light harmonies, Ray and Dave's vocal line traced by Rasa Davies' wordless falsetto, are bursting with emotion. When most of the instruments drop away at 1.20, the effect is effortlessly vivid — two lines where Davies' performance is both nonchalant and impassioned. The result is wonderfully, enchantingly sad, made more so perhaps by the knowledge that The Kinks will never again sound so refined or so right.

Twenty years later, Davies told Jon Savage that although 'Big Sky' was one of his favourite songs, he was dissatisfied with The Kinks' recording of it. "Maybe I wasn't the right person to sing it," he said.[16] "Knowing I got the image across and the fact that a lot of people like the song is enough. But my performance is really bad. . . . It just wasn't recorded properly . . . "[lxxv] Davies has habitually deflected attention away from the personal nature and commercial failure of *TKATVGPS* by claiming either that the songs suffered from his inexperi-

---

[16]Davies told Jonathan Cott he would like to hear 'Big Sky' intoned by the rather more messianic sounding Burt Lancaster.

ence behind the mixing desk ("those songs are demos really, pure demos . . . They're good ideas but not executed properly. I was lacking a producer . . . "[lxxvi]) or that he deliberately under-recorded them ("I wanted a record that would not necessarily get airplay but would be played for friends and at parties — just play the record like playing a demo. I achieved that and it didn't get any airplay at all. It became a cult record as a result."[lxxvii]) 'Big Sky', so scintillating in design and execution, gives the lie to both these evasions.

Coincidentally, the final two songs recorded for *TKATVGPS* were also the only two The Kinks carried over into their live set at the time, where they would be introduced as numbers from "an LP we had out but few people bought" or "an album we had out called *The Village Green Preservation Society*. I don't know if you've ever heard of it." (The scattered, half-hearted applause that usually followed these announcements indicates most gig goers had not). Live, 'Big Sky' ("as opposed to pig sty") received the same kind of heavy rock punishment meted out to 'Last Of The Steam-Powered Trains'. At the Fillmore West in 1970 the song resembles Hendrix's 'Hey Joe', with its lethargic power chords and longwinded rolls across the tom-toms. Ray Davies shouts over the din, struggling to make those beautiful words heard above his brother, who is busy kilowatting the song to death with his guitar. Horrible.

Sadly, this was the end of the road for 'Big Sky'. After 1972 The Kinks dropped it from their live set, never to return. Neither Ray Davies nor Dave Davies has sung it since. A pity; it is one of The Kinks' — and the pop era's — finest two minutes and fifty seconds, eternally fresh and, like the Big Sky himself, ultimately consoling and inspiring.

Sitting By The Riverside

'Sitting By The Riverside' was probably recorded in July 1968; it was definitely performed by The Kinks during their appearance on *Late Night Line-Up* at the end of the month. Yet oddly it was absent from the twelve-track version of *TKATVGPS* prepared by Ray Davies for release in September. "This is a fishing song," he said in November. "I went fishing a lot when I was about eight,"[17] and it may be that the song's inclusion on the finished album owes more to considerations of pacing and flow than to its nominal subject matter. By the illustrious standards of its predecessors, 'Sitting By The Riverside' is a slight, if charming, piano and accor-

---

[17]Shades of *Coming Up For Air* again. George Bowling's happiest childhood memories are of days spent fishing, an image that in part supplies the novel's title.

dion (i.e. Mellotron) shuffle, two minutes to pause and cast your metaphorical eye on the waters before turning the record over.

However, being Ray Davies, there is something awry in this picture of riparian bliss. Anxiety shrouds the riverbank. The singer needs to be calmed and pacified, not just loved. He sounds exhausted, utterly passive, happy to let the water pass him by — at last he can close his eyes. But when he does so, a dizzying rush of instruments — memories, or fears — threatens to overwhelm him. The second of these gentle cacophonies (at 1.55), mixed with the melancholy image of a willow tree, is an instance of Davies' production and songwriting skills combining to produce something richly impressionistic. At the song's close, the fog clears and the singer is left surveying the view with a bottle of wine, suspended half way between a harmless sunny afternoon's lazing and a more insidious self-regarding torpor, like the phenomenal cat at its journeys' end, high in a tree, eating itself forever.

"The best tracks to put last are the ones that lead you somewhere," said Davies in 1993. 'Sitting By The Riverside' looks ahead to the album's conclusion via the unreliable gallery of people and memories that comprise *TKATVGPS*'s second half, a book of pictures the singer will contemplate and eventually reject.

Animal Farm

Side two of *TKATVGPS* opens with its most unapologetic pop song, and a favourite of the group. "I still get shivers when I listen to it," admits Pete Quaife, which isn't to say that things went smoothly in the studio. "There was a big fight about 'Animal Farm'. I thought the bass should be playing the piano introduction as well. Both Ray and Dave threw a hissy fit and said no. So it's not there. I was a bit angry and sour about that one." There is no evidence of this contretemps on the finished record. Quite the opposite in fact: 'Animal Farm' sounds light and joyful.

Of course, the song has sadness tucked away inside it. "This was just me thinking everybody else's mad and we are all animals anyway — which is really the idea of the whole album," Davies told Bob Dawbarn, going on to describe himself as "just a city dropout."[lxxviii] Once again, the singer seeks sanctuary in the past, this time on 'Animal Farm', the pastoral idyll under a wide (Big?) sky where he was happy, life was simple and people could be trusted. In the dream, his "little girl" is safe at his side — not like the big, bad, half insane world where dreams are easily snuffed out and from which she, presumably, is missing.

Mick Avory remembers The Kinks recording 'Animal Farm' (and possibly one other song from this period) in the larger environs of Pye Studio 1, normally used by Pye artists and producers when orchestral backing was required. Certainly, 'Animal Farm' has a noticeably bigger sound than much of the rest of the album, with plenty of reverb applied to the drums, percussion and the tack piano that picks out the song's opening riff. A Mellotron has been expertly manipulated to forge the realistic "string" parts that fill out the track, while Quaife's zooming bass line in the opening bars suggests the Davies brothers got the arrangement right. Finally, Davies' terrific vocals, uncommonly lusty in the opening lines of the verses, put the seal on a skilled and infectious group performance.

Ray Davies seems to have been fond of 'Animal Farm'. The song featured on *Four More Respected Gentlemen* and both versions of *TKATVGPS*. In addition to selecting it to announce the second side of the finished album, Davies recycled its introduction in a song called 'Nobody's Fool', the theme to the second series of Adam Faith's television show *Budgie*.[18]

---

[18]Although The Kinks never recorded the song, the lachrymose 'Nobody's Fool' is worth tracking down. The version released as a single on Pye (!) in 1972 is by a group with the quite possibly pseudonymous name of Cold Turkey, whose vocalist sounds uncannily like Dave Davies.

Village Green

Ray Davies hoarded 'Village Green' like no other song in his growing catalogue.[19] "It's all very camp, isn't it?" he said when it was finally released, noting that the track "was done eighteen months ago and was originally going to be the title for the album."[lxxix]

Davies had a point. Musically, 'Village Green' is very camp and its archness is only partially alleviated by its surroundings; in comparison to its sister song 'The Village Green Preservation Society', written and recorded nearly two years later, it is distinctly two-dimensional. An acetate exists of 'Village Green' where Davies' vocals are even more mannered and sarcastic than on the finished track.[20]

'Village Green' was recorded at Pye in November 1966 or February 1967.[21] The Kinks' ranks, still with a

---

[19]Although 'Village Green' was never considered for *Four More Respected Gentlemen*, the song was first officially released in May 1967 on a French EP called *Mister Pleasant* (along with the title track, 'This Is Where I Belong' and 'Two Sisters'). It also appeared on a Spanish EP prior to *TKATVGPS*.

[20]This version of the song lacks orchestral accompaniment, and could well be a demo for the prospective arranger.

[21]Although a version of 'Village Green' was recorded in November 1966, in *X-Ray*, Davies dates this session to February 1967. "When Robert [Wace] heard 'Two Sisters' he smiled for the first time in what seemed like many months and said that I had taken my writing into another class." (Pg 336) It may be that overdubs were added to the basic tracks in February.

notably *Face To Face*-like drum sound, are swelled by Nicky Hopkins' harpsichord and an arrangement by David Whitaker that features oboe, cello, viola and piccolo. (Dave Davies stated in a 1967 interview that his brother's solo album would feature "an orchestra and things like that."[lxxx]) Despite Whitaker's impressive C.V., which ranged from film soundtracks to arrangements for The Rolling Stones and Brigitte Bardot, the Davies brothers reportedly fell out with him for failing to interpret their musical wishes to the letter (or note).[22] The finished track lacks the tidiness of 'Two Sisters', sounding cluttered in places, the extra instruments jostling for attention with The Kinks' hearty backing vocals and a somewhat uncertain group performance.

Musically maladroit it may be, but the ever-present literary sensibility of *TKATVGPS* finds its fullest expres-

---

[22]Strings are noticeably absent from The Kinks recordings of the next two years. As Doug Hinman suggests, "the hiring of an arranger and string players was an expensive proposition probably not seen as worthwhile by the frugal Pye Records executives." And besides, Davies had high hopes for the "cost-effective" Mellotron, with its tape loops of horn and string sounds. Nevertheless, the yen for real violins, violas etc. seems to have stayed with Davies. In April 1969, he flew to Los Angeles to produce the *Turtle Soup* LP for The Turtles. Howard Kaylan: "He brought in a large orchestra, strings and horns. . . . He thought that the orchestrated sound of the Turtles and that Hollywood production value that he had been missing on his records he could put onto ours. It was a strange thing."

sion in 'Village Green'. The song's portrait of a van-
ishing rural idyll places it firmly in an English pastoral
tradition that stretches back from Shakespeare to William Blake ('The Ecchoing Green' from *Songs Of Innocence*, 1789), William Wordsworth ('Michael', 1800)
and, in the twentieth century, Orwell (yes, him again),
whose symbolic use of Winston Smith's dreams of a
Golden Country in *Nineteen Eighty-Four* is intended to
evoke just this literary heritage ("Winston woke up with
the word Shakespeare on his lips.")[23] In 1982, the director, actor and former boy genius Orson Welles offered
this definition of the English pastoral for the cameras
of the BBC's *Arena*: "I think Shakespeare was greatly
preoccupied with the loss of innocence. I think there
has always been an England, an older England, which
was sweeter and purer, where the hay smelt better, and
the weather was always springtime, and the daffodils

---

[23]Did Ray Davies go through a phase of reading Orwell? Much of
the landscape of Davies' 1970's *Preservation* work suggests a famil-
iarity with the totalitarian dystopia of *Nineteen Eighty-Four*.
TKATVGPS contains a song called 'Animal Farm'. And then there
are the repeated echoes of *Coming Up For Air*. "Orwell had nostalgia
himself, certainly," writes Bernard Crick in his biography of the
writer, "but in balance, not to excess as he deliberately portrayed
in Bowling [in *Coming Up For Air*]. So the nostalgia of the novel as
a whole was deliberately ambivalent. . . . There are so many good
things in the past that we should preserve, the novelist says, but
clinging to the past is no solution." (Crick, Pg 376)

blew in the gentle, warm breezes. You feel nostalgia for it in Chaucer, and you feel it all through Shakespeare. I think he was profoundly against the modern age."[lxxxi] And lo, there are The Kinks on the cover of *TKATVGPS*, strolling through just such a pastoral scene.

Where there was paradise, there is paradise lost. Here are a few lines from 'The Deserted Village' by Oliver Goldsmith, first published in 1770:

> *Sweet smiling village, loveliest of the lawn,*
> *Thy sports are fled, and all thy charms withdrawn;*
> *Amidst thy bowers the tyrant's hand is seen,*
> *And desolation saddens all thy green . . .*
> *Here, as I take my solitary rounds,*
> *Amidst thy tangling walks and ruin'd grounds,*
> *And, many a year elaps'd, return to view*
> *Where once the cottage stood, the hawthorn grew,*
> *Remembrance wakes with all her busy train,*
> *Swells at my breast, and turns the past to pain.*

It could be Ray Davies in a powdered wig.

Davies has frequently said that the 'Englishness' of his lyrics at this time, the profusion of cups of tea and country houses, was a product of The Kinks' five-year banishment from America, but the English sensibility of Davies' songwriting has a deeper, older root. If 'Village

Green' is — dread phrase — quintessentially English, it is not because of its literal use of images of oak trees, church steeples and so on, but because it employs these images to suggest innocence has been lost. This is the very kernel of the English pastoral theme, a retrospective, self-renewing pessimism. Things will never be as good as they used to be. For Davies, The Kinks' US ban was surely the proof, not the cause.

In 'Village Green', and throughout *TKATVGPS*, the pastoral and the personal have become entwined. "I sought fame," says the singer, and the suggestion is that by seeking fame, he feels he has contributed to the despoiling of the village. He has abandoned love and, in doing so, has left behind a lifeless place, fit only for gawping Americans and Daisy's husband Tom, who now owns the grocery, the pithiest and funniest detail of the entire album. The singer will return, he and Daisy will be reunited, laughter will once again be heard around the green. By its final verse, the song has become a study in pathetic self-deception, an impossibly perfect scene no better or more realistic than the "rare antiquities" snapped by those darn tourists. You can't go home again, said Thomas Wolfe; Davies appears deluded enough to believe he can.[24]

---

[24]As pointed out by Ken Rayes, Daisy and Tom are the names of the destructive married couple in F. Scott Fitzgerald's *The Great*

Why did Davies cling on to 'Village Green' for so long before letting it be heard? It may be that he had reservations about revealing his "ideal place, a protected place" — "the worst thing I did was inflict it on the public. I should have left it in my diary."[lxxxii] But he also saw 'Village Green' as a starting point for something new, not just the Village Green concept and the distinctive songs that would spring from it, but the type of work he could produce outside the strictures imposed on him by The Kinks and the demands of the hit machine. However, the moment passed; in some respects, Davies' decision to include the song on *TKATVGPS* can be seen as a capitulation, not just to The Kinks but also to his wavering self-confidence. By the time it was finally released, 'Village Green' was confirmed as Ray Davies' personal parable, and its lost innocence belonged to no one but himself.

Starstruck

'Starstruck' was recorded by The Kinks in July 1968 and included on both the twelve and fifteen-track versions of

---

Gatsby, a novel that relocates the pastoral tradition to the USA. For more parallels between the book and the album, see 'The 'Village Green' and 'The Great Gatsby' — Two Views of Preservation' in *Living On A Thin Line*, Rock'n'Roll Research Press, 2002.

the album. Thirty-three years later, reflecting on the song in the liner notes for *This Is Where I Belong*, Ray Davies professed to being baffled at 'Starstruck''s inclusion on *TKATVGPS*. "It is strange to think of this song being recorded by The Kinks," he wrote, "because it is definitely a song that should be on somebody's solo album".[lxxxiii]

Sure enough, 'Starstruck' appears to have little in common with the Village Green theme, although as a warning on the perils of fame and the big city, it bears some relation to other Davies songs of the period, such as 'Village Green', 'Berkeley Mews' and 'Polly'. "The lyrics are self-explanatory. It's just something that happens," said Davies at the time.[lxxxiv] As Johnny Rogan notes, it could be that the softly censorious lyric is addressed to a groupie, although the politeness of Davies' vocal suggests otherwise.

Davies has claimed that the musical inspiration for the song came from his love of Motown groups such as The Temptations and The Four Tops. While it's possible to hear echoes of, say, 'It's The Same Old Song' (a minor British hit for The Four Tops in 1965) in Davies' melody (and the snap of Mick Avory's snare drum), in truth a person could listen to 'Starstruck' a thousand times before spotting the connection between Fortis Green and Detroit. It just sounds so much like The Kinks — the familiar line-up of acoustic guitar, bass, drums, piano and Mellotron, all those jolly "ba ba ba' "s and handclaps.[25]

In fact, 'Starstruck' sounded so inimitably Kinky, it was released as a single in America, Germany and parts of Scandanavia. A basic promotional film was shot in late 1968 at Waterlow Park, Highgate, in which The Kinks half-heartedly mime and goon about in the winter chill, Ray Davies' breath forming clouds as he sings along. The ground is muddy and the leaves are off the trees. The film plays like a bedraggled monochrome lantern show of the photographs shot on Hampstead Heath a few months earlier. Pete Quaife is just weeks from quitting the group.

Phenomenal Cat

Prior to 1968, The Kinks had only ever flirted with psychedelia — the influential 'See My Friends', the backwards tapes of 'Autumn Almanac' — but *TKATVGPS* contains two numbers, 'Phenomenal Cat' and 'Wicked Annabella', that sail unusually close to the cosmic wind blowing through British pop at the time. According to Robert Christgau, who had a low tolerance

---

[25]Fans of 'Starstruck', take note: the mono mix of the song is a few seconds longer.

for English "impersonal artsiness", the songs "might have been turned out by some Drury Lane whimsy specialist".[lxxxv] Yet while both tracks have the trappings of psychedelia, neither could be said to be truly psychedelic. Ray Davies was too smart (and too uptight) to deal in either unconditional bliss or plain lysergic infantilism.[26]

Davies referred to 'Phenomenal Cat' as a nursery rhyme, and superficially the song is a snug fit with such Brit psych classics as 'The Gnome' by The Pink Floyd or The Fleur De Lys' 'Gong With The Luminous Nose'.[27] The underground adopted, or co-opted, figures like Edward Lear and Lewis Carroll, both for the perceived

---

[26]In 2002, Sanctuary Records, missing the point for sound commercial reasons, included 'Wicked Annabella' and 'Phenomenal Cat' on a compilation album called *Haunted: Psychedelic Pstones II*, alongside nuggets from such forgotten talents as The Orange Seaweed, The Glass Menagerie and The Flying Machine.

[27]'Phenomenal Cat' most closely resembles the work of The Kinks' Pye label mate Donovan, whose double LP *A Gift From A Flower To A Garden* was released in April 1968. One disc was for adults, the other for children. The album came packaged in a dark blue two-pieced box, printed in full colour on the outside and inside, and included an orange folder containing twelve inserts for the twelve songs on the children's record. Each insert was a different colour, with the lyrics and a drawing illustrating each song. It is difficult to imagine tight-fisted Pye sanctioning such extravagance happily; later that year, they would turn down Ray Davies' request for a double album.

trippiness of their work and the romantic dream of childhood it evoked. Ray Davies shared the British psychedelic scene's pastoral idealization of lost youth; where he differed was in the belief that, with a child-like view of the universe (and enough L.S.D.), one could get back to that walled garden. "Maybe *Village Green Preservation Society* was my psychedelic album," Ray Davies told *The Onion* in January 2002. "I withdrew into my little community-spirited . . . my trivial world of little corner shops and English black-and-white movies. Maybe that's my form of psychedelia."[lxxxvi]

'Phenomenal Cat' is a funny mix of Mellotron, electric guitar and tambourine, with Mick Avory playing what sounds like the small practice kit he had had made for Kinks rehearsals. The song's decorative introduction was created by holding down the Mellotron keys and letting its "flute" tapes spool through. Ray Davies is double-tracked throughout, while the cat himself is a speeded-up Dave Davies, fabricated by slowing down the track's master tape. In common with other Mellotron-heavy Davies productions such as 'Lavender Hill' and 'Mr. Songbird', it is thought 'Phenomenal Cat' was recorded in late 1967, by which time the psychedelic bandwagon was rolling out of town. Would it be too much to interpret the 'Strawberry Fields Forever' flute-trills, faux-naïve fabulist lyrics and magic singing cat as vaguely satirical? After all, 'Last Of The Steam-Powered

Trains' would pull a similar trick with the conventions of R&B. And this was a group whose guitarist, though not averse to wearing a preposterous Noddy hat and conducting interviews with 'LOVE' and 'DAVE' written on his knuckles, gave short shrift to the beautiful people in the press ("There's something very strange about a flower scene in Acton — people walking around with flowers up their noses, cream on their hair and riding on a number 233 bus. I mean, it's not very beautiful, is it?"[lxxxvii]) and whose bassist, in late 1967, said this:

"I just let the whole flower people, L.S.D., love thing flow over my head. I just laughed at it. The trouble is it changed a lot of good blokes, who everybody rated, into creeps. Instead of expanding minds, L.S.D. seemed to close minds into little boxes and made a lot of people very unhappy. You still can't beat going to the pictures, a couple of pints and a fag. The Kinks all agree that Sunday dinner is the greatest realisation of heaven."[lxxxviii]

No wonder people thought they were unfashionable. Whether modish or mocking, the psychedelia of 'Phenomenal Cat' is all surface. The lyric is another Ray Davies rumination on the dangerous charm of the past. The cat who perches in a tree, eating himself forever, is the same ambiguous figure who sits idly drinking wine by the riverside all day, who flicks compulsively through old family photo albums, who lives in a museum and is going insane. The Phenomenal Cat, fantastically, has flown from Cowes to Kathmandu and unlocked the very secrets of the universe; now all he wants to do is wallow and eat, eat and wallow, until he ends up feeding on himself. Like many of those around the Village Green, the cat has found his rest, but at a price.[28]

Ray Davies thought enough of 'Phenomenal Cat' to consider it for *Four More Respected Gentlemen* and both versions of *TKATVGPS*. The song also makes a significant reappearance in *X-Ray*. Late in the book, the narrator is stalked by the same (literal) cloud of dark despair that afflicts 'Raymond Douglas'. "All he had to do was to look the cloud in the face and smile at it," RD tells him. "Then it would become discouraged and disappear . . ."[lxxxix] When the predatory cloud visits the narrator at night, he disperses it by putting on *TKATVGPS* and playing 'Phenomenal Cat'. Like 'Mr. Songbird', "I let the record play continuously, knowing that it would protect me from the darkness." The narrator falls asleep, content that "the Phenomenal Cat would watch over

---

[28]Ken Rayes speculates that 'Phenomenal Cat' may be Davies' caricature of the businessman Allen Klein. "I cite Davies's account in *X-Ray* of their first meeting where he compares him to rotund comedian Lou Costello, and his portrayal of Klein's braggadocio concerning his famous clients and all of 'the places he had been' ". (*Living On A Thin Line*, Pg 163)

me."[xc] (Again, it can't be ruled out that Davies is having some mild fun here).

This idea of 'Phenomenal Cat' as an audible smile in the encroaching gloom is supported by the last and subtlest of its original production touches. As the track ends, Ray Davies and the Phenomenal Cat harmonize for the first time, high and low together, until the cat passes on his little song and fades away, leaving Davies to sing the wordless refrain alone, like the grin on the face of Lewis Carroll's Cheshire Cat as it gradually disappears.

All Of My Friends Were There

Another song retrieved from the pages of Ray Davies' diary, 'All Of My Friends Were There' was inspired by a real on-stage humiliation.

"It was an R&B concert and I had a temperature of 104 but they asked me to do it because there was a contract. I had lots and lots to drink and I thought 'It doesn't matter'. The curtains opened and all my friends were sitting in the front row. . . . It was a terrible night and I thought I would write a song about it."[xci]

In the finished song, the drama unfolds with the woozy logic of a bad dream. The event has become a tawdry showbiz story of persecution, stage fright and booze, set to a music-hall gallop in the verses, contrasting with the lilting, wistful waltz of the choruses (not dissimilar to 'Young And Innocent Days' on *Arthur*). "I was thinking the other day about some of the things that poor Mick Avory had to play," Davies told Peter Doggett. "All he wanted to be was a jazz and blues drummer, and I brought in all these weird songs."[xcii] Avory and The Kinks acquit themselves on the album's trickiest number, albeit with some slight, appropriate awkwardness.

'All Of My Friends Were There' takes perverse delight in Davies' mortification. The song, like its singer, is a tragicomic jumble of paranoia, panic and deception. Are these "friends" really my friends, or friends of friends, or not friends at all? When will it be over? When can I get back to normal? In the final verse, Davies changes tack, reprising the Village Green theme of return to the past. After struggling through his comeback gig, the singer goes to a café he used to visit in happier times, where everyone was his friend and he could be himself; or at least, that's how he remembers it. The song ends with Davies once again gazing at the (imaginary?) view, passive, dazed, exhausted. Finally, he doesn't care.

Like 'Sitting By The Riverside', 'All Of My Friends Were There' was recorded in the summer of 1968, but not included in Davies' original track listing for *TKATVGPS*. "If I'd done that song today, it would have been A&R'd off the album," Davies said. "But sometimes you need minor gems like that to set up other songs."[xciii] Again, it seems that the last-minute inclusion of 'All Of My Friends Were There' was a case of Davies deciding the album needed a track for reasons of continuity alone. But it is a fine Kinks recording, and one that offers a glimpse of its author's troubled mind.

Wicked Annabella

Whereas 'Phenomenal Cat' represents the "something 'far-out' in the nursery" strand of British psychedelia, 'Wicked Annabella' is as close as The Kinks ever got to the genre's other notable manifestation, the Freak Out. Guitars growl and shriek, vocals are menacing, double-tracked and whispered. As such, the song is perfectly suited to the younger Davies' particular talents. "This is rather a crazy track," said Ray Davies. "I just wanted to get one to sound as horrible as it could. I wanted a rude sound — and I got it."[xciv]

To some extent, Ray seems to have turned 'Wicked Annabella' over to Dave and the other members of The Kinks. The younger Davies' vocals are suitably threatening and the group's playing on the finished track is loud and live. Pete Quaife remembers the song as an example of that summer's temporary spirit of collaboration between Davies and the rest of the group.

During the breakdown from 1.12 to 1.19, Quaife picks out a snatch of Bach's 'Jesu, Joy Of Man's Desiring'. "It popped into my head while we were going through it and I just threw it in. It just so happened — serendipity — that I ended it at the right point and went back into 'Wicked Annabella'." Davies retained the improvisation for the finished recording.

'Wicked Annabella' is another pure Village Green character song, a pen portrait of the local witch, although it should be noted that the tales of Annabella's wickedness are all second-hand and are being employed to keep children in their beds and out of the wild woods. In this respect, it is another psychedelic nursery rhyme like 'Phenomenal Cat', though too scary (and noisy) for a lullaby. As the recording draws to its extended close, the tape is doused in echo and reverb, becoming a suitably infernal cauldron of feedback and disembodied laughter.[29]

The Kinks never performed 'Wicked Annabella' outside the studio, but in recent years it has become one of the highlights of Dave Davies' live set. "Wooah! Bogeyman's coming!" he shouts at the start of the great version to be found on *Rock Bottom, Live At The Bottom*

---

[29]The mono mix of 'Wicked Annabella' has more reverb and more volume.

Line, and proceeds to tear it up, proving thirty years on that the song now belongs entirely to him.

Monica

Another character song squirreled away at the end of Side Two, 'Monica' is one of a line of Kinks calypsos that began in 1965 with 'I'm On An Island' and would go on to include 'Apeman' and 'Supersonic Rocket Ship'. Fortunately for 'Monica' and us, Davies mostly eschews the cod-Jamaican delivery he would later employ on such tunes. Over a pleasant syncopated backing of acoustic guitar, congas and organ (no bass until the second verse), he croons a sort-of love song to the village prostitute. "I like the way I did 'Monica'," he told *Crawdaddy*. "I didn't actually say she was a prostitute. . . . If you say somebody is a prostitute or a hooker you're restricted."[xcv]

Recorded in the spring of 1968, 'Monica' is the flimsiest thing on *TKATVGPS*, but as far as Davies was concerned, the song was a keeper from the beginning. He selected it for *Four More Respected Gentlemen* and both editions of *TKATVGPS*, and The Kinks recorded it twice for the BBC, on July 1st and July 9th 1968. In 2001, the second of these takes was released on *BBC Sessions 1964–1977* and is chiefly remarkable for Pete

Quaife's bass fluff at 1.23 and a different, non-faded ending, which is to say it isn't very remarkable at all.

One gets the impression that Davies thought he had been very clever with 'Monica', maybe even subversive. "It's about a prostitute and the BBC has played it," he bragged to *Melody Maker* when the album was released, although perhaps he should have been more circumspect about admitting it. Four months later, Auntie Beeb would have her revenge by banning The Kinks' new single 'Plastic Man' for its shameless use of the word 'bum'.

People Take Pictures Of Each Other

"I'm not very witty at all. I feel intensely about a lot of things but it might come out in a funny sounding way," said Ray Davies in late 1969. "If you can make a funny song and then have one very hard line, you reach people. That's just a construction thing."[xcvi]

'Last Of The Steam-Powered Trains', 'Big Sky', 'All Of My Friends Were There': *TKATVGPS* has quite a few Ray Davies songs built on this artful blueprint — the sting in the tale, the one very hard line — but none of them does it quite like 'People Take Pictures Of Each Other', and no other Village Green track packs the same emotional punch. In its final minutes, the album's mix of frivolity and despair achieves a new level of intensity. Davies programmed the song as the LP's finale on both the twelve and fifteen-track versions, and may even have written it with that purpose in mind (viz. the schematic reappearance of the oak tree from 'Village Green' and the family snaps from 'Picture Book'). It works. Set against the songs that have preceded it, 'People Take Pictures Of Each Other' is both a conclusion and a confession; the entire lyric is the long "very hard line" that Davies hopes will connect. Where 'Picture Book' concluded with a bang, 'People Take Pictures Of Each Other', and *TKATVGPS*, ends with a whimper: please, don't show me any more.

Davies told Mark Breyer and Rik Vittenson that the song was inspired by a wedding he and Rasa had attended. "The guy was in the navy . . . and he put a flag up in the back garden . . . and they all stood there and they took a picture. And then she got the camera and took a picture of him . . . and he got the camera and took a picture of her. . . . That's where that came about. I just got the line and then built on that."[xcvii] 'Raymond Douglas' expands on this in *X-Ray*: "That lyric sums up the way I feel about the world of photographic images . . . I think that pictures only encourage nostalgia. I like to remember people the way they were. . . . The camera may not lie, but it is not entirely honest."[xcviii]

'People Take Pictures Of Each Other' resonates far beyond its photographic inspiration, with the kind of authorial empathy and acuity most poets or novelists would give their eyeteeth for. As Rob Chapman writes, the lyric "offers a cameo of human beings validating a transitory existence and also serves as a metaphorical postscript for the swinging '60's".[xcix] That it does so while set to a silly vaudeville piano vamp is a mark of Ray Davies' peculiar genius. The tune dashes up and down the ivories, nearly falling over itself in the process. The Kinks keep on top of the arrangement — just about — while Davies sounds out of breath and on edge. There is something neurotic about the wordless vocal tics that punctuate the song, and something desperate about the singsong round the piano as the track fades. The summer has passed by, childhood and freedom have vanished, love has been stolen away. You used to matter to someone, but now you don't. You might as well sing. It's all you've got — that, and your photographs.[30]

---

[30]In its original stereo mix, 'People Take Pictures Of Each Other' concludes with a trad jazz line-up blowing a ragtime number — That's All, Folks! — but it was removed for copyright reasons at the last minute, presumably because Davies used a pre-existing recording rather than hire a jazz band. It can be heard as an extra track on the current British edition of the album. There are in fact three mixes of the song in circulation: the original stereo mix with coda

At the end of the song, Davies brilliantly restates his album's double-edged preoccupation with the past, four lines that are as spare as a haiku. In 1975, he would close *Schoolboys In Disgrace*, and bring the curtain down on the era of Kinks' conceptual productions like *Preservation* and *Soap Opera*, with the determined self-admonishment of 'No More Looking Back'. But in 1968, things are less clear-cut and more pensive. At the conclusion of *TKATVGPS*, Davies displays a vulnerability that is deeply affecting. In the years that followed, the leader of The Kinks would hide behind hard rock, Big Ideas, and a self-consciousness about the 'craft' of songwriting which often stifled his work. Here, he sounds exhausted and desperate but maybe on the verge of the freedom alluded to so longingly throughout the album. All he has to do is look away . . .

Thrillingly, 'People Take Pictures Of Each Other' has the distinction of being the only track on the original album to attract a contemporary cover version — El Salvadorian group Los Comets who, in 1969, recorded the song as 'Hay Que Respetar . . . '[31]

(2.22), the standard stereo mix without coda (2.10) and a slightly longer mono mix (2.14).

[31] The contemporaneous 'Days' received the easy listening treatment from Petula Clark and James Last. The majority of *TKATVGPS* cover versions originate in the late 80's and 90's and American indie artists (and dyed-in-the-wool 60's obsessives) like Matthew Sweet

Ironically, for one so sensitive to the despotism of the photographic image, ("It makes events which should be ambiguous turn into absolutes, and it disallows personal interpretation,"[c]) Ray Davies cannot resist putting a gloss on the pictures that adorn the sleeve of *TKATVGPS*. "When one of the founder members leaves, the band is dead. Once you lose the thing — the four originals getting together, going through it together, forming the band together — once that goes, the group is a different group. That picture signs it off."[ci]

('Big Sky'), Jason Falkner ('Wicked Annabella'), Young Fresh Fellows ('Picture Book'), Yo La Tengo ('Big Sky' and 'Animal Farm'), etc etc.

Chapter Three — Pictures In The Sand

In a sense, Ray Davies' final selection and sequencing of tracks on *TKATVGPS* is his greatest achievement. After a year of piecemeal recording sessions, he created a coherent, intelligent work. The LP is a concept album in the truest sense of that much-abused term, held together not by narrative and rock star hubris but by sound, imagery and ideas. "The subtext to the whole record was more interesting than the songs themselves,"[cii] says the young narrator of *X-Ray*, but he is misguided (and so is Davies for putting such slyly defensive words into his mouth). The secret of the record is that the songs create a subtext by virtue of being mostly wonderful songs. In later Davies concept works, starting with *Arthur* the following year, too many tracks sound like they've been shrunk or expanded to fit the premeditated subject matter.[32] And as any weary listener to *Preservation Act 2* will tell you, you can't whistle subtext.

Davies was an inveterate and compulsive writer (taking into account his contributions to *At The Eleventh Hour*, Kinks recording dates and record releases, it can be estimated that he composed at least twenty songs in the first three months of 1968 alone) and the themes of the album are the themes of most of his work at this time. As Andrew Sandoval notes, many Davies songs from late 1967 to late 1968 would fit easily onto *TKATVGPS*, largely because Davies was principally writing about himself.

"Over the years I have left a lot of songs off records," Davies told Peter Doggett in 1993. "I get bored with songs — not because they're bad, but because I've moved on. You always feel you should record the most recent thing you've written."[ciii] There follows a survey of Ray Davies songs recorded by The Kinks in the principal period the group was working on *TKATVGPS*

---

[32]To be fair, *Arthur* was a commission / collaboration with Julian Mitchell and Granada TV, until Granada pulled out at the last minute.

which did not make the final cut of the album, some of which remain obscure. Although, technically, recording began in November 1966 with 'Village Green', for obvious reasons I have not included tracks from *Something Else By The Kinks* nor the attendant singles and flipsides (so no 'Waterloo Sunset' or 'Autumn Almanac').

The Kinks were so productive in 1968 that they also found time to record two fabulous Dave Davies singles ('Lincoln County' b/w 'There Is No Life Without Love', and 'Hold My Hand' b/w 'Creeping Jean') plus a few tracks for Davies' still unreleased solo album (including 'Crying' and 'Do You Wish To Be A Man?'). I do not have space to discuss those songs here, but it can only be hoped that this fine album will finally receive a legal release in the coming year or so.

Finally, The Kinks recorded three instrumentals in this period. 'Easy Come, There You Went' and 'Spotty Grotty Anna' are studio jams or warm-ups. Both circulate on bootleg, although 'Spotty Grotty Anna' briefly received an official release in the early 1980s, against Davies' wishes. The track was named in honour of London's most notorious groupies ("Every group knew her," remembers Pete Quaife, "especially the Dave Clark Five"). The third instrumental remains unheard in any form, although Ray Davies has spoken warmly of it in interviews. Its title? 'Mick Avory's Underpants'.

She's Got Everything

If it sounds like a relic from the glory days of The Kinks, that's because it is. 'She's Got Everything' was more than two years old by the time it appeared as the b-side of 'Days'. Recording took place during the spring of 1966, although the song may have received additional overdubs for its belated 1968 appearance. The track is an unreconstructed rave of the sort not minted by The Kinks since 'Till The End Of The Day', with a Dave Davies guitar solo that is both timeless and utterly ridiculous.

'She's Got Everything' is not a product of the Village Green concept in any of its incarnations, but Ray Davies' decision to release it when and how he did is interesting. In the summer of 1968, despite having many more recent Kinks tracks to choose from, he selected a song that, even when it was recorded, must have sounded old-fashioned. The tracklisting for *TKATVGPS* was still in flux, and it is clear that Davies did not want to waste any potential candidates for the finished album as b-sides. It seems appropriate, however, that the nostalgia of 'Days' should be matched with a song that recalls The Kinks in their hunting jackets and leather boots — and, given the late date of its recording, one that is almost a knowing pastiche of the sound formerly made by that group (as is the manic absolutism of the lyric).

Lavender Hill

'Lavender Hill' was recorded in August or September 1967, at roughly the same time as 'Autumn Almanac', and features some prominent use of Mellotron and backwards tapes. One of the projects Davies was reported to be working on in 1967 was an album of songs about London but although there is a Lavender Hill in Battersea, South London, made famous by the Ealing comedy *The Lavender Hill Mob*, Davies makes it clear in the song's opening lines that his Lavender Hill is a make-believe place, a sun-drenched refuge where songbirds sing and people have tea and biscuits, and dream of daffodils and summer breezes. The idea of Lavender Hill as Davies' very own promised land is reinforced by the reference to sugar and milk i.e. milk and honey. It is another wistful song of escape by the beleaguered leader of The Kinks.

After its fleeting appearance on *The Great Lost Kinks Album*, this lovely song has never been reissued. The only place to hear it (and 'Pictures In The Sand', 'Rosemary Rose', 'Misty Water', 'Where Did My Spring

Go?', 'Till Death Us Do Part' etc etc) is on one of the numerous CD bootlegs containing the *GLKA* tracks.[33]

Rosemary Rose

Yet another song to mention treasured holiday snaps (taken, as in 'People Take Pictures Of Each Other', at the age of just three), 'Rosemary Rose' is a Ray Davies miniature from late 1967 or early 1968. In a few short lines, Davies sketches out the thoughts and feelings of a parent as they ponder their teenage daughter's growing pains, caught somewhere between liquorice and cigarettes. At well under two minutes, the track is notable for Nicky Hopkins' baroque harpsichord work and, of course, the reappearance of Rose, the Davies sister who emigrated to Australia with her husband Arthur, and the inspiration for *Face To Face*'s 'Rosie Won't You Please Come Home'. It sounds transitional, half way from a Ray Davies solo offering to a Village Green character vignette. Officially unavailable for nearly thirty years, 'Rosemary Rose' is another suppressed gem from *The Great Lost Kinks Album*.

---

[33]All these songs are available in perfect sound quality on the *'Neue Revue' Great Lost Kinks Album* (HTSLP 340016 P) and Japanese *Secret Sessions* (Phenomenal Cat 63/72) bootlegs. The author needs to remind you that bootlegs are illegal and does not condone their sale or manufacture. Even listening to them makes you a bad person.

Mr. Songbird

There is a famous Swiss story about a depressed man who goes to see the doctor.

"Doctor," says the man, "I am miserable. Everything is desperate and nothing I do seems to make it better. Please help me."

"You're in luck," says the doctor. "The great clown Grock is in town. Go and see him perform. He's so funny! He could cheer anybody up, however low they're feeling."

The man looks infinitely sad. "But doctor," he says. "I am Grock."

'Mr. Songbird' is Ray Davies' version of the story of Grock (it was a London pop paper cliché at the time to refer to The Kinks' frontman's "sad clown face"). The song is about the power of music, not just to those who listen to it but also those who make music like Davies himself. When Mr. Songbird sings, everyone's problems seem very small. Like the dark cloud in *X-Ray* that is dispersed by a few plays of 'Phenomenal Cat', a little melody will keep the devil at bay — but don't doubt for a minute the devil is there. The song's concluding phrase is Davies' 'one hard line' technique in full effect, the punch line of the Grock story. There is real fear in it.

'Mr. Songbird' is a sublime Davies creation; its blithe melody and toe-tapping arrangement being both perfect accompaniment and cover for the concerns of the lyric. Nicky Hopkins' Mellotron flute part is faultless, blocking out chords in the verses and trilling the song-bird responses in the chorus.[34] Pete Quaife and Mick Avory play with real lightness and care. Davies' vocal may be double tracked, but it is unusually sincere and direct. Why the decision was made to release 'Won-derboy' as a single when The Kinks had a track like this in the can is a mystery. 'Mr. Songbird' is one of the high points of *TKATVGPS*.

Or rather, it should have been. Probably recorded in late 1967 (another potential solo number?) Davies selected it for *Four More Respected Gentlemen*, and then did so again for the twelve-track *TKATVGPS*. The track was duly released in Europe as part of that album. But in the October interim while Davies was frantically re-vising the LP, 'Mr. Songbird' and 'Days' were dropped. 'Days' had been freely available as a single but, excepting its inclusion on *The Great Lost Kinks Album*, 'Mr. Song-bird' was inexplicably shelved for the next thirty years. In 1998, the song finally received a full release on the

---

[34]Andrew Sandoval notes the similarity between Hopkins' Mellotron work on 'Mr. Songbird' and Zal Yanovsky's guitar part on 'You're A Big Girl Now', a single by avowed Kinks' favourites The Lovin' Spoonful.

British reissue of the album, although, to date, it remains unavailable in the USA. What a waste. 'Mr. Songbird' is far too good — no, great — a record to be forgotten, least of all by the man who sang it.

Berkeley Mews

In August 1970, The Kinks scored their biggest hit since 'Sunny Afternoon' in 1966. By his own admission, no one was more surprised by this than Pete Quaife. He had left The Kinks partly because he felt the group was winding down; few people seriously expected Ray Davies to deliver another top ten single, let alone a smash. "And then along came 'Lola'," Quaife says wryly. He was even more surprised when he turned the record over and played its flipside. "I thought, is that me? Wait a minute — it is me!"

'Lola' was backed with 'Berkeley Mews', a track re-corded by the original line-up of The Kinks some two and a half years earlier, in late 1967 or early 1968. After Nicky Hopkins' barrelhouse piano introduction, the whole group crashes in, somewhat sluggishly pounding away, with Mellotron, handclaps and even a saxophone joining in for the song's high-kicking coda (Davies' vocal, incidentally, is quite brilliant, teetering between pain and pride). It is one of the oddest productions of the Village Green era, but still a classic Kinks recording.[35]

Like 'Misty Water', Davies initially liked 'Berkeley Mews' enough to shortlist it for *Four More Respected Gentlemen* but changed his mind for *TKATVGPS*. The song's broken-hearted account of a drunken one-night stand sounds distinctly autobiographical. Berkeley Mews was (and still is) located round the corner from Pye Records at Marble Arch, although Davies may simply have liked the genteel, champagne-and-chandeliers resonance of the name. Like 'Starstruck', the lyric has little to do with the Village Green concept; unlike 'Starstruck', the candid 'Berkeley Mews' failed to scrape onto the finished *TKATVGPS*.

In the UK, 'Lola' was huge, selling in comparable numbers to The Kinks' biggest hits from the sixties. Ironically, the single's success meant that 270,000 Brit-

---

[35]'Berkeley Mews' was first released in July 1969 on an American promotional Kinks LP, *Then, Now and Inbetween*. It may be that the track was subject to some additional work just prior to this. It is a noticeably heavier production than anything else recorded by The Kinks in 1968. The guitars are loud and then there is the underused saxophone player — just a few bars at the end of the song. Certain Dave Davies tracks (e g 'Mr Reporter') received belated brass over dubs during the May and June 1969 sessions for *Arthur*, so it is possible the brief saxophone part at the end of 'Berkeley Mews' was added at this time — the instrument is certainly an anomaly in The Kinks' Village Green sessions.

ish homes got to hear 'Berkeley Mews' as well — roughly a quarter of a million more than the album that spawned it.

Polly

Recorded in late 1967 or early 1968, 'Polly' is the sound of The Kinks firing on all cylinders, combining the familiar Davies theme of the not-so-innocent abroad in the big city with a full, coherent group sound of the sort not found on either *Something Else By The Kinks* or *TKATVGPS* ('Love Me Till The Sun Shines', 'Funny Face' and 'Wicked Annabella' are all rave-ups written by and / or showcasing Dave Davies). It proves that, when he wanted to, Ray Davies could produce Kinks records in this period that were simultaneously smart *and* noisy. In the case of 'Polly', he may have felt the song was a throwback to *Face To Face* and 'Big Black Smoke', hence its consignment to the b-side of 'Wonderboy'. "I didn't like 'Polly' at all," Davies admitted to Jon Savage. " 'Pretty Polly Garter', that's all I wanted to say really, I don't know why . . . "[civ] Nevertheless, Davies thought enough of the track to select it for *Four More Respected Gentlemen*.

In fact, there was a tragic source of inspiration for 'Polly' and 'Big Black Smoke'. "I knew a girl who was like that," Davies told Savage. "She ran our first fan club.

She died of junk.""cv Once again, the pastoral yearning for home and lost innocence in The Kinks records of this period has a personal foundation.

In one other obvious respect, 'Polly' is closely related to the pure Village Green character concept, Polly Garter being the name of a character from Dylan Thomas's *Under Milk Wood*. It should be noted, however, that Davies only borrowed the name. His Polly has little or nothing to do with the Polly Garter of *Under Milk Wood*.[36] Pretty Polly was also a brand of popular ladies' stockings — the song was actually called 'Pretty Polly' on early pressings of the single — so there is at least one extra joke hidden in her surname. If Polly's are the legs on the advertising hoardings, it explains why those all those people can't be wrong and she is such a hit with the fellas.

Wonderboy

The Kinks recorded 'Wonderboy' (or 'Wonder Boy' — the title has varied for thirty-five years) in early 1968. It is that rare animal in The Kinks' catalogue from the Village Green era: a potentially great song undermined by its treatment in the studio. Down in the Pye base-

---

[36]One of the play's other principal characters is called Captain Cat, but there is little that is phenomenal about him. Oh, and he isn't a cat.

ment, Davies' inspiration seems temporarily to have deserted him. The production is flat, there are few dynamics in the arrangement and The Kinks sound listless and unconvinced by the song (which, according to Pete Quaife, they were). The combination of a facile clip-clop rhythm, weedy background vocals and Nicky Hopkins' one-speed keyboard arpeggios produces something unmistakeably kitsch, a style Davies had flirted with on his records but usually pulled back from. Unfortunately, this time he confirmed and compounded the offence by singing "as if recently stunned by a heavy blow from a blunt instrument," as Chris Welch put it in *Melody Maker*. It was all too much. Initially, we know Davies was proud of his new composition; but for whatever reason, when the time came to capture 'Wonderboy' on tape, he buried it.

The pity is that 'Wonderboy' conceals one of Davies' most insightful and compassionate lyrics. Supposedly penned during a vodka-fuelled long night of the soul, it sees Davies offering both despair and hope to a newborn baby. At the time, the Denmark Productions court case was still dragging on (as it would continue to do throughout most of 1968) and Davies was caught up in a doomed love affair, the same one that would inspire the sweet sorrow of 'Days'. 'Wonderboy' tries to find wisdom in the mire. Life is what you make it, Davies says to the baby boy, but even if you make a mess of it, that's all part of the wonder of being alive. Life may be lonely but that's no reason to be sad, because the rest is up to you.

Although 'Wonderboy''s lyric suggests mistakes are all part of life's rich pageant, whoever made the final decision to issue the track as a single, it was not a good one. Within weeks of its half-expected failure on the charts, the record had been pretty much disowned by Ray Davies. "It should never have been released," he told Keith Altham in August. After a few promotional appearances and the unsuccessful package tour of April 1968, the song was dumped from The Kinks' live set and the group never performed it again. To date, Davies has not revisited it in his solo live shows nor, in contrast to 'Days', has the song been much covered by other artists (Eddi Reader being the only notable exception). It seems that 'Wonderboy', like much of *TKATVGPS*, reminds Davies of the beginning of an unhappy period in his life, personally and professionally.[37] "It felt that

---

[37]If Davies ever intended 'Wonderboy' for *Village Green* or *TKATVGPS*, he quickly changed his mind. Following its failure as a single, the track was abandoned and never seriously considered for any new Kinks album, not even the aborted *Four More Respected Gentlemen*. As a single, the recording was mixed in mono, and that is how it has remained on nearly all its subsequent compilation appearances. The rare stereo mix is awful, obscuring the vocal track for most of the song, and was only included on a few budget LP collections in the late 1960's and early 1970's. To my knowledge, it has never been issued on CD.

(sic.) the people who bought the record had not under-stood my own little subtext," he writes in *X-Ray*. "They were buying a Kinks record. To me it was a cry for help."[cvi]

'Wonderboy' has a reputation as John Lennon's fa-vourite Kinks record, but Lennon never complimented Davies on the song directly: the story came back to him via Grenville Collins, who had heard from a third party that Lennon had been spotted in a restaurant or night-club (the tale varies in the telling) demanding that the single be played over and over again. "I guess that ap-proval from my peers meant that 'Wonder Boy' had not been a complete mistake," wrote Davies many years later.[cvii] The story may be true or it may not, but aside from the sympathy one feels for Lennon's fellow diners or dancers — Kinks fans or no — the anecdote speaks volumes about the group's diminished status in the spring of 1968. The Kinks' new single had unceremoni-ously flopped, and Ray Davies was reduced to taking comfort from the second-hand patronage of a Beatle.

Did You See His Name

'Did You See His Name' was one of the songs Ray Davies wrote in early 1968 for the television series *At The Eleventh Hour*. "They phoned me on a Monday morning wanting the song by Wednesday," he said. "I

ANDY MILLER

tried to use topical ideas."[cviii] Davies drew inspiration
for lyrics from stories he found in the newspaper. In
the case of 'Did You See His Name', the song both
relates an incident of petty theft and also the effect the
newspaper report of the offence has on the thief i.e. he
is so ashamed he kills himself (in "his gas-filled maison-
ette" — a typically deft Davies detail).

"My GP, Doctor Aubrey, was an old-school doctor,
in the Boer War and all that," Davies said. "I was looking
through various stories for 'Did You See His Name' in
the local paper because I had to write a story about a
man with a tragedy in his life. I saw an obituary for
Doctor Aubrey, and it made me feel a real shit for
getting stories from ordinary people."[cix]

The Davies compositions from *At The Eleventh Hour*,
as noted above, were not performed by The Kinks, but
by the singer Jeannie Lamb and a small orchestra. The
Kinks' version of 'Did You See His Name', therefore,
is an oddity. As far as we know, the group attempted
no other songs from the series. It was hastily recorded in
spring 1968 and is something of a bare bones production
with Ray playing organ, clocking in at a mere 1.55.
Although it is unlikely the track was ever seriously considered for *TKATVGPS*, it was submitted to Reprise as
part of *Four More Respected Gentlemen*. However, when
FMRG was cancelled, 'Did You See His Name' remained on the shelf until the 1972 release of Reprise's

The Kink Kronikles collection. Nearly thirty years later, the song made its UK debut on *BBC Sessions 1964–1977*.

Days

In the last few years, 'Days' has become something of a pop standard, one of those much admired and covered songs whose provenance may be unclear in many people's minds. 'You Really Got Me' and 'Waterloo Sunset' are synonymous with The Kinks; but after thirty years of radio play, its use in adverts and the sad death of Kirsty MacColl (who scored a top twenty UK hit with the song in 1989), 'Days' belongs to a wider audience. It articulates how we would all like to remember our friends, our lovers and our lives: gratefully, and without regret. It is Ray Davies' wisest song.

As recounted earlier however, the circumstances of 'Days'' recording in May 1968 were as turbulent as any in The Kinks' short but volatile life up to that point. The resulting track should be the sound of raised voices and rising panic. Instead, the song shines a light into the darkness and finds solace there.

'Days' is one of Davies' great performances, spine-tingling in the bridge as he sings to hold back the night ("It's like saying goodbye to somebody, then afterwards feeling the fear — you actually are alone," he later said).[cx] However, like 'Wonderboy', the production is rather flat and it takes a few listens to distinguish between instruments — acoustic and electric guitars, bass, harmonium and piano, with Nicky Hopkins' trusty Mellotron duplicating string sounds. Mick Avory's drumming builds at the back of the mix, really only coming alive in the stirring lead-in to the final chorus (2.00 — 2.05). The track ends with the same sort of gentle crescendo that occurs twice in 'Sitting By The Riverside', the sound of nostalgia rising up. However, unlike the later song where the cacophony threatens to overwhelm the singer, in 'Days' it leads to resolution, finishing in a harmonious D major chord, and the sense of an ending promised by Davies' lyric.

Sales of 'Days' were respectable rather than spectacular. By The Kinks' high standards, this was a low-key success. "I still have a lot of faith in our latest single 'Days'. If we like a record and like making it, it becomes a successful venture," Davies told *Record Mirror*, with a degree of selective amnesia. "Some releases are slow and perhaps this is one of them."[cxi] The Kinks worked it accordingly, recording the number twice for BBC Radio[38] and promoting it on *Top Of The Pops*, *Late Night Line-Up* and *The Basil Brush Show*. In fact, 'Days' is the

---

[38]On 1st July and 9th July 1968. The first of these performances is available on *BBC Sessions 1964–1977*.

---

ultimate grower, thirty-five years and counting. On first listen, it is a rather underwhelming production, certainly compared to the firework display of hits that preceded it. Part of its modern popularity is due in no small measure to its inclusion on years of budget Kinks' compilations.

In October 1968 Davies dropped 'Days' from the final version of *TKATVGPS*. This was despite the song's obvious lyrical ties to the Village Green concept and its provisional inclusion on both *Four More Respected Gentlemen* and the twelve-track version of the album. It may be Davies felt that, with his choice limited to fifteen tracks, 'Days' had already been made available as a single and could be discarded. However, this does not explain why, save for a valedictory performance for BBC 2's *Pop Goes The Sixties* on New Year's Eve 1969, he and The Kinks then ignored one of their classic songs for the next twenty years. 'Days' received its first significant live outing on 18th April 1988 in Berkeley, California. Perhaps in the intervening years, the song grew on Ray Davies like it grew on everyone else (or *because* it grew on everyone else — 'David Watts' and 'Stop Your Sobbing' only returned to The Kinks' live repertoire in the early 1980s after hit cover versions by The Jam and The Pretenders respectively).

By the early 1990s, 'Days' was established as a popular classic, and was finally acknowledged as such by its writer. The track has been reinstated on the most recent British edition of *TKATVGPS*. The Kinks rerecorded the song for *To The Bone* in an almost identical arrangement to the original single, and it has become a fixture of Ray Davies' solo shows, where it is usually preceded by the 'Daze' / 'end of the group' story. This may be an example of artistic license on Davies' part, but so what? 'Days' is, after all, about coming to terms with your past. When Ray sings 'Days', he and the audience share their own nostalgic communion; one of the most expressive and compassionate pop has to offer.

Pictures In The Sand

Unlike its photographic partners, Ray Davies has never deemed 'Pictures In The Sand' worthy of an official release. Although the track was recorded in the spring of 1968 (a Pye acetate exists coupling the track with 'Picture Book'), it was never considered for *TKATVGPS* or for *Four More Respected Gentlemen*. In 1973, Reprise issued the song on *The Great Lost Kinks Album*, presumably against Davies' wishes, but since that album's deletion a couple of years later, 'Pictures In The Sand' has never reappeared, and all attempts to include it in subsequent reissue programs have been frustrated.

Davies' apparent reluctance to let 'Pictures In The Sand' be heard by a wider audience is mystifying. The track is one of his most beguiling creations, a classic Kinks confection of the late 1960's. Over a polite backing of acoustic guitar, bass, drums, harmonica and organ, Davies sings of sipping tea on the promenade and writing messages on the beach, before leading the chorus into a balmy seaside sing-a-long (even bringing them in with an "all together now!"). The singer knows he is wasting his time trying to draw his love, because pictures in the sand will always be washed away, but he does it anyway. The track draws to a close with a fade reminiscent of the bouzouki-led theme to the 1964 movie *Zorba The Greek* (a.k.a. 'Zorba's Dance', a top ten British hit for Marcello Minerbi in 1965).

'Pictures In The Sand' shares the shoulder-shrugging lethargy of 'Sitting By The Riverside', although without the latter's air of defeat. In fact, Davies had attempted to record a similar song during the sessions for *Something Else By The Kinks*. 'Sand On My Shoes' shares its melody and arrangement with 'Tin Soldier Man', but its lyric is similar in several respects to 'Pictures In The Sand'. However, 'Sand On My Shoes' does not really go anywhere (it comes across as an inferior retread of 'Sunny Afternoon') and it is easy to see why Davies scrapped it and refined the concept in later songs.

'Pictures In The Sand', meanwhile, would have fitted easily on *TKATVGPS*. Only Ray Davies knows why it remains relatively unheard.

ANDY MILLER

Misty Water

Another Village Green character cameo. Over the years Ray Davies has written his fair share of lyrics about the demon alcohol, but none quite so fizzy as 'Misty Water'. Pitched at the other end of the social realist scale from 'Alcohol' or 'When Work Is Over', the song is a cartoon of Maria and her daughters and their fondness for a spot of the misty stuff (and 'misty glade' is a euphemism for pub worthy of Dylan Thomas). The singer shares the family's taste for fog. Things go better, Maria is lovelier, hell, *everything* is lovelier, when seen through a misty haze — in fact, it's paradise! He is not just drunk on alcohol, but on his memories.

Musically, 'Misty Water' is upbeat and underdeveloped — mostly piano and organ until 2.07, when Dave Davies appears with a half-hearted holler and a power chord or two. The lead and background vocals seem to disagree about exactly who likes misty water, although this may be a deliberately befuddled mix-up. The track was recorded in May 1968 and was selected for *Four More Respected Gentlemen*. However, when that album was cancelled, the song disappeared, surfacing only briefly on *The Great Lost Kinks Album* and the withdrawn 10" ep that accompanied PRT's contentious *The Kinks' Greatest Hits/Dead End Street* compilation in 1983. It has not been reissued.

Till Death Us Do Part

Recorded in September 1968, 'Till Death Us Do Part' is another unjustly neglected minor classic. Written for the big-screen adaptation of the successful television comedy series (and at one stage considered as a Ray Davies solo single — see 'Plastic Man'), to date the song has only ever been officially released on *The Great Lost Kinks Album*. A version using The Kinks' backing track with one Chas Mills on vocals was included on the film's soundtrack LP.

The original TV series of *Till Death Us Do Part* featured an East-end bigot, Alf Garnett, and his long-suffering wife, daughter and son-in-law. The film depicted the Garnett family living through the London Blitz. However, for his song 'Till Death Us Do Part', Ray Davies ignored the hectoring tone of the series and the film. Alf Garnett's abrasiveness is nowhere to be found. Instead, Davies penned a tender observation of the state of holy wedlock, revealing the lost little man behind Garnett's loud-mouthed façade. The Kinks recorded the song as a slightly unsteady pub serenade, with banjo and mournful trombone accompanying one of Davies' prettiest melodies and a touching vocal performance. He catches the vulnerability and faint hopelessness of the lyric. Life has left me behind, so let's accept the small consolation we have — to be together till death (and beyond). The effect is both anti-romantic and rather moving. And is that Mrs. Davies on backing vocals . . . ?

'Till Death Us Do Part' is currently only available on bootleg.

When I Turn Off The Living Room Light[39]

Another song written for television. In early 1969, a year after *At The Eleventh Hour*, producer Ned Sherrin invited Davies to contribute to his new series *Where Was Spring?*. This was not a revue like the previous show, but an episodic romantic comedy starring Eleanor Bron and John Fortune, albeit with a satirical edge. As noted above, The Kinks recorded five songs for the programme, which were accompanied on screen by Klaus Voorman's illustrations. The group itself never appeared in front of the cameras.

---

[39]Pedant's corner: When the song was first released on *The Big Ball* and *The Great Lost Kinks Album*, it was called 'When I Turn Out The Living Room Light', probably the result of a US clerical error — Davies sings "off" and the Reprise tape log shows the title as such. In 2001, *BBC Sessions 1964–1977* upheld the ignoble *TKATVGPS* tradition of misprinting song titles, not once but twice; the sleeve notes refer to 'When I Turn Out The Living Room Light', while the cover lists the track as 'When I Turn Off The Living Room Lights'.

'When I Turn Off The Living Room Light' is one of the most popular "lost" Kinks tracks, but over the years the opening verse has caused a degree of consternation among some fans, a few erroneously interpreting it as anti-Semitic. One should recall the context in which the song was written. Whereas *At The Eleventh Hour* had required Ray Davies to lift stories from newspapers, his songs for *Where Was Spring?* were concerned with the vicissitudes of life, love and sex, the themes of the programme. It was down to Davies to fulfil the brief of that week's show, hence song titles like 'Let's Take Off All Our Clothes' and 'Darling I Respect You'. In the case of 'When I Turn Off The Living Room Light', the lyric is wilfully, exaggeratedly seedy. Lust conquers all, even the prejudices of the singer. The small but crucial shift of emphasis in the final verse — *we* turn the light off because *we're* uptight and ugly — is a twist worthy of Randy Newman, but a careless listener might miss the irony entirely, and a few have done. What is certain is that, heard cold on a Kinks' compilation album and with no knowledge of its TV origins, the song retains its power to amuse, unsettle and confuse in equal measure.

The Kinks recorded 'When I Turn Off The Living Room Light' at the BBC's Riverside Sound Studios in Hammersmith on February 4th 1969. The track was first released in April 1970 on a Reprise mail order sampler album called *The Big Ball*, before being briefly revived for *The Great Lost Kinks Album* in 1973. It finally received a Ray Davies-sanctioned release on *BBC Sessions 1964–1977*. Although the song is emphatically not a Village Green-era composition, I include it (and the few other film and TV songs that still exist) because I think it shows that, when freed from the pressure of producing hit singles for The Kinks, Davies was still on a roll. Far from collapsing under the failure of *TKATVGPS*, his muse was in great shape. As we shall see, 'Plastic Man' was both an aberration and a turning point.

Davies himself thought the song was an insubstantial effort and was unimpressed by its popularity. "Americans seem to love that song," he told Jon Savage. "I don't know why they like it. It's like a lot of American things, films or whatever — it's all over in the first five minutes, and the rest of it is filling."[cxii]

King Kong

The proto-glam production, the monster title, the Marc Bolan-like vocal warble . . . 'King Kong' seems to be a wicked parody of Bolan's group T-Rex, until you remember that The Kinks recorded 'King Kong' at least eighteen months before 'Ride A White Swan' provided T-Rex with their first hit single. All of which makes the thumping 'King Kong' even more of a puzzle. Like 'Plastic Man', an elaborate production has been applied to a two-dimensional song. Everyone wants to be as big, powerful and famous as King Kong — and that's that. It is not known if the track was recorded in October 1968 (with 'Big Sky' and 'Last Of The Steam-Powered Trains'), in March 1969 during the 'Plastic Man' sessions, or at some point in-between. However, so removed is 'King Kong''s lyric from the concerns of *TKATVGPS*, it may be that the song, like 'Plastic Man', was recorded with a view to a specific single release. The Kinks issued it as the b-side of 'Plastic Man' and recorded nothing like it again.

Plastic Man

'Plastic Man' is an awful record and an admission of defeat. What's more, Ray Davies knew it. "This record has outgrown what a pop record can be. This record has more love for people," he bullshitted in *Melody Maker*. "It's probably not the greatest song I've ever written and not the greatest song I'll ever write. But it's the only song I could have written at this time. Even though I hated it when I first heard the acetate! But I think it could be a hit."[cxiii]

There's the rub. Post-*TKATVGPS*, a hit was what
The Kinks desperately needed. They knew it and so
did the rest of the pop world. As Derek Johnson wrote
in his review of the single in *NME*, "a lot hinges on
this record, because The Kinks have been out of the
public eye recently — and their last couple of discs
haven't exactly been world-beaters . . ."[cxiv] In *Melody
Maker*'s Blind Date column, Keith Moon once again
analysed The Who's former rivals with sardonic accu-
racy. After listening to just a few bars of 'Plastic Man',
he shouted out the naffest thing he could think of —
"Tony Blackburn!"[40]

"They've done some nice things. 'See My Friend'
and 'Waterloo Sunset' but they haven't done much
since. I've liked some of the songs on their albums. I
don't think they've got a lot together . . . No, that's not
a lot of bottle. That means, not a lot of good."[cxv]

How galling this must have been for Ray Davies.
After a dry spell of their own, The Who were back in
the top ten with 'Pinball Wizard'. Ominously, it her-
alded the birth of Pete Townshend's oft-discussed *Deaf,
Dumb And Blind Boy* rock opera, now renamed simply
Tommy. Here were The Kinks, whose own visionary

---

[40]Tony Blackburn is a famous British disc jockey who remains as
naff today as he was in 1969.

concept LP had already sunk without trace, knocking out a single that sounded like a cheap and gutless rehash of 'Dedicated Follower Of Fashion' — and perhaps beginning to get the sense that *Tommy* was going to clean up. 'Plastic Man' stalled outside the top thirty.

"I hate it," Davies has said. "It was a desperate attempt. Somebody said that we'd got to have a record out to do the tour, and that's what they got."[cxvi]

In early 1969, Davies was in a bind. Pye was reluctant to release a single from *TKATVGPS*, thereby sealing the album's flop status. With a heavy irony, the record company was also pressuring him into issuing The Kinks' recording of 'Till Death Us Do Part' as a Ray Davies solo single. "Ray has wanted to do some solo singing, too," Dave Davies told *Beat Instrumental* when his new single 'Hold My Hand' was released. "He wrote the song for the Alf Garnett movie and they naturally wanted him to bring out a record on it because it would be a good seller. But he somehow just didn't want to do it. I think he's a bit afraid of being typecast as a solo singer."[cxvii] No doubt Ray Davies was fuming. He had let The Kinks have the album that was originally intended to be his grand personal statement, and then watched as Pye promptly abandoned it. Now they were asking him to launch a solo career with a film soundtrack tie-in. Not surprisingly, he refused.

A compromise was reached. The Kinks would record a new, specially written song for release in the spring; better that than a repeat of the 'Wonderboy' fiasco a year earlier, when Davies had been coerced into finding a single in the tape vault. He had produced hits under record company pressure before — 'Set Me Free', for instance — but up in the huge, empty house in Borehamwood, Davies faltered badly. 'Plastic Man' is entirely without warmth or charisma, a rank impersonation of The Kinks delivered through gritted teeth, as fake and phony as its subject. Unbelievably, it has the distinction of being the first Kinks single recorded and mixed on an eight-track desk, but the extra studio polish does little to hide the resentment at its core.

In the press, Davies declared that 'Plastic Man' marked the end of his solo ramblings under the guise of The Kinks' name. "What is important is that it's the first 'group' record that has been made for a long time," he said penitently. "It certainly expresses my brother Dave's feelings. But it's a part of each one of us."[cxviii] Shortly afterwards, the part of 'Plastic Man' that was Pete Quaife left The Kinks for good.

Nevertheless, the plan nearly worked. 'Plastic Man' was warmly received by disc jockeys and music journalists, who welcomed back what sounded like the 'brilliant piss-takers' of yore. John Dalton was swiftly ushered back into the fold and television appearances were lined up. A promotional film was shot. It looked like The Kinks were on course for a sizeable hit. And then the BBC instituted its ludicrous ban for the single's use of the word 'bum' and 'Plastic Man' rapidly turned to dust, leaving Davies complaining about "a BBC monopoly" in *Record Mirror*: "I suppose it's doing as well as any record could be expected to do that's been out for four weeks and hasn't had a television plug," he sniffed[cxix]. As a result, the bespoke single sold even fewer copies than 'Wonderboy'. The Kinks turned to Granada TV, *Arthur* and America, for preservation.

'Plastic Man' marks the moment in Ray Davies' career when his plans for an artistic life outside The Kinks came to a twenty-five year halt, only partially interrupted by his 1985 television film *Return To Waterloo*.[41] Had 'Plastic Man' been a hit — or even had it been any good — Davies might yet have been able to divide the strands of his work, as he had wanted to in The Kinks' better days. After the failure of *TKATVGPS*, 'Plastic Man' represented his final opportunity to separate Ray Davies and The Kinks, but it too failed. Instead, from hereon in Davies tried to fuse his personal musical

---

[41]The *Return To Waterloo* soundtrack LP was credited to a solo Ray Davies. However, it was intended to be a Kinks album (three tracks had already appeared on 1984's *Word Of Mouth*), until Dave Davies objected and refused to have anything to do with the project.

ambitions with The Kinks' brand. Sometimes this approach succeeded — *Arthur*, *Muswell Hillbillies*, half of *Preservation Act 1*. On other occasions, the results were disastrous. After *Schoolboys In Disgrace*, the balance swung back to the group, or at least what Davies thought people wanted from a rock group. The Kinks became a polished arena act, cranking out the hits and tracks from shiny-but-patchy new albums. By the late 70s, those albums were going top ten on Billboard and selling hundreds of thousands of copies. It took a decade, but having been denied the opportunity in the 1960's, Ray Davies finally broke America. It was a hollow victory. By that point, The Kinks had become a plastic phenomenon, and the intricacies and sensibilities of the 60's group that bore their name had long since perished. They were fixed in the pantheon of Classic Rock™, well respected, doing the best things so conservatively.

Where Did My Spring Go?

The failure of *TKATVGPS* affected Ray Davies deeply. After the humiliation of 'Plastic Man', he threw himself into the writing and recording of *Arthur*, a project that was a commission from Granada Television. Locked away in his new mansion, we know Davies struggled to write. Granada's last-minute decision to cancel the television play left him with half of a finished product, a soundtrack but no movie to go with it. While *Arthur* has its share of marvellous songs, the production is more generic than on the previous few Kinks albums, and the self-indulgence of late 60's rock has started to impinge both on the group's sound and Davies' writing. The Kinks' unique subtlety is beginning to drain away.

And then, in late 1969, the doors to America swung wide open. Not only was The Kinks' performance ban rescinded but, thanks to a self-consciously serious rock press and Reprise's assiduous (if patronising) 'God Save The Kinks' campaign, *Arthur* was received as a work of genius. *Rolling Stone* ran two reviews of it in one issue. "A masterpiece on every level," said Mike Daly, while Greil Marcus called *Arthur* "the best British album of 1969." "It shows that Pete Townshend still has worlds to conquer, and that The Beatles still have a lot of catching up to do,"[cxx] he wrote, a sentence that must have put Marcus on the Davies Christmas card list for years to come. Although *Arthur* was not a hit, and The Kinks comeback tour of America was often a shambles — the musicians had never even used stage monitors before — the basis was there for a career revival. The Kinks had a future again. Over the next few years, the tension between Davies' desire to carry on exploiting the group and his highfalutin musical ambitions would result in some very uneasy listening. Ironically, the wit and decorum of *TKATVGPS* would soon seem like a golden age.

So 'Where Did My Spring Go?' seems like a fitting way to end this book. The song was written for the second episode of *Where Was Spring?* (and recorded at the BBC's Riverside Sound Studios on Jan 28th 1969) but in all other respects it is the perfect coda to the story of *TKATVGPS*. Under a conspicuously pastoral title, its lyric confronts the album's theme of ageing with humour and honesty. The group's performance is tight and well thought-out and Davies' restrained production, though no doubt the result of circumstance, allows the song to breathe. He sounds properly agitated as he reels off a list of his lost properties; teeth, hair, shoulders, chest, hormones, energy, skin, muscles, liver, heart, bones, not to mention 'go'. Even as the lyric drolly subverts the romantic clichés of walking in the rain and candlelit nights of lovemaking, Davies sings the lines in a panic-stricken yelp, while The Kinks whip up a nerve-jangling racket behind him. The singer has been used, employed, destroyed . . . such existential humour would not find another outlet in British pop until the arrival of The Smiths in the early 1980s.[42]

Davies considers this performance of 'Where Did My Spring Go?' to be a demo and nothing more, hence

[42]In their fascination with the lives of 'ordinary people', and a style that is literate, witty and empathetic, Morrissey and Davies have much in common.

its current obscurity (*The Great Lost Kinks Album* and bootleg only), yet as far as we know, he has never tried to rerecord the song. Sometimes, however, a demo catches something a more polished production might miss or obliterate. In the case of 'Where Did My Spring Go?', the January 1969 recording captures the last gasp of the original Kinks in their prime. It shows Ray Davies could have carried on writing songs and making records in the vein of *TKATVGPS*. For whatever reason — Pete Quaife's departure, the changing rock scene, Davies' need for new challenges, commercial opportunities for The Kinks in the USA, the intensely personal letdown of *TKATVGPS* — he chose not to. Perhaps he had simply gone as far as he could with these versions of the group and himself.

The Kinks were dead — long live The Kinks.

Epilogue — The Echoing Green

Days they'll remember all their lives . . . Have you ever wondered what The Kinks will tell their children and grandchildren years hence? About the days when they used to sing and play — and people screamed and applauded. We're lucky enough to be able to appreciate the Kinks now, when they are at the height of their stardom. Lucky, aren't we?

Fabulous 208, September 7th 1968

In Russia, nostalgia is regarded as an illness. Or at least it used to be. In the good old days.

Simon Munnery, The League Against Tedium

The *TKATVGPS* revival began within months of the album's release and summary disappearance. As noted, the American music press acclaimed The Kinks as prophets without honour in their own land, an accolade Ray Davies was all too happy to accept. British magazines quickly fell in behind their cool older cousins; an early issue of *Zigzag* carried a retrospective appreciation of The Kinks, accompanied by a photograph of Ray Davies on Hampstead Heath on that sunny August afternoon in 1968. Although the album was unavailable for many years, its tracks were spilled across cheap compilations like *Golden Hour Of The Kinks*. Those in the know compiled their own tapes of the LP.

The age of the compact disc opened up many groups' back catalogues to exploration and exploitation — and few groups' back catalogues have been exploited quite so thoroughly as that of The Kinks. Listeners who only knew the group from their 60's hits discovered an album full of songs as good as those golden oldies, but one that was fresh and unfamiliar. Like Nick Drake's *Bryter Layter* or *No Other* by Gene Clark, classic album status was bestowed on this lost artefact, pulling in yet more admirers and converts (and back catalogue sales — in a reversal of fortune, these days *TKATVGPS* is reportedly The Kinks' best-selling original album).

Thirty-five years on, tourists still flock to the Village Green. The trauma of the LP's creation has mostly been forgotten, and the darkness beneath its surface overlooked. "I wonder if it's not what it says on that

VILLAGE GREEN PRESERVATION SOCIETY

album, but the images it conjures up, that people like," Davies said recently.[cxxi] The final irony — *TKATVGPS*, Ray Davies' attempt to picture the conflicting emotions of nostalgia, has become a nostalgic snapshot in its own right, The Kinks wandering through the long grass on a summer's day, forever.

Ray Davies, meanwhile, persisted with The Kinks until he could go no further. "Maybe that's one reason The Kinks have suffered down the years," he said in the early 90s, "I've slipped all these oddball songs that don't really fit the band on to the albums. It's something I'm trying not to do now."[cxxii] At the time of writing, The Kinks have not played a gig for nearly eight years, and Ray Davies is still putting the finishing touches to his first solo album.

The Kinks may be gone but *The Village Green Preservation Society* goes on forever. As I wrote at the start of this book, Ray Davies' songs are about growing up and growing old — the problem of being alive. Davies was twenty-four when he conjured up the magic of *TKATVGPS*; soon he will be sixty. When he was young, he wrote and recorded two dozen miraculous songs. Out of them he fashioned an album that has no equivalent in pop, rock or whatever we call it in the twenty-first century, one that is weightless and profound, vintage and modern. Year-by-year, it reveals new colours and new depths. It is not simply a snapshot of The Kinks

· 139 ·

at their peak, and not just an exhibit in the museum of classic rock, but a work whose relevance and perceptiveness grow more acute as the years pass and the shadows lengthen. Out of his past, Ray Davies dreamed the future. We keep listening to *TKATVGPS* because it is the album of a lifetime — his and ours.

God save the Village Green.

Select Bibliography

The Kinks

Kink, An Autobiography, Dave Davies, Boxtree, 1996
X-Ray, The Unauthorized Autobiography, Ray Davies, Viking, 1994
Waterloo Sunset, Ray Davies, Viking, 1997
You Really Got Me, An Illustrated World Discography Of The Kinks, 1964–1993, Doug Hinman with Jason Brabazon, Rock 'n' Roll Research Press, 1994
Living On A Thin Line: Crossing Aesthetic Borders With The Kinks, edited by Thomas M. Kitts and Michael J. Kraus, Rock 'n' Roll Research Press, 2002
The Kinks, Neville Marten and Jeff Hudson, Sanctuary, 2001
The Kinks Kronikles, John Mendelssohn, Quill, 1985
The Kinks, The Sound And The Fury, Johnny Rogan, Elm Tree Books, 1984

The Complete Guide To The Music Of The Kinks, Johnny Rogan, Omnibus Press, 1998
The Kinks, The Official Biography, Jon Savage, Faber and Faber, 1984
The Kinks Kompanion, Jerome Wallerstein, 1998

Additionally, interview and archive material was drawn from four sources: the British Library's newspaper and periodicals department at Colindale, North London; the National Sound Archive collection at the British Library, Euston; the personal collections of Bill Orton and Russell Smith of the Official Kinks Fan Club; and the extensive on-line archive of Dave Emlen's excellent Kinks website, which can be found at http://kinks.it.rit.edu/.

Secondary Reading

Albion, The Origins Of The English Imagination, Peter Ackroyd, Chatto & Windus, 2002
The English Village Green, Brian Bailey, Robert Hale Limited, 1985
Songs Of Innocence And Of Experience, William Blake, Oxford, first published 1794, definitive edition published 1967
England Is Mine, Pop Life In Albion From Wilde To Goldie, Michael Bracewell, HarperCollins, 1997
Beat Merchants, The Origins, History, Impact And Rock Legacy Of The 1960's British Pop Groups, Alan Clayson, Blandford, 1995
George Orwell: A Life, Bernard Crick, Secker & Warburg, 1980
The Deserted Village, Oliver Goldsmith, 1770
'The Howlin' Wolf' in *Lost Highway, Journeys And Arrivals Of American Musicians*, Peter Guralnick, David R. Godine Publishers, 1979

The Mojo Collection, edited by Jim Irvin, Mojo Books, 2000

Mystery Train, Images Of America In Rock 'n' Roll Music, Greil Marcus, Dutton, 1975

Coming Up For Air, George Orwell, Victor Gollancz, 1939

Nineteen Eighty-Four, George Orwell, Secker & Warburg, 1949

Revolution, The Making Of The Beatles' White Album, David Quantick, Unanimous, 2002

Under Milk Wood, A Play For Voices, Dylan Thomas, Orion, first published 1954, definitive edition published 1995

Finally, I must make special mention of two particularly important and influential titles. Anyone who sets out to write this kind of study does so in the shadow of Ian MacDonald's superb *Revolution In The Head, The Beatles' Records & The Sixties*, Fourth Estate, 1994. If you haven't read it yet — why not? Svetlana Boym's *The Future Of Nostalgia*, Basic Books, 2001, provides this book with one of its epigraphs. Her multi-faceted account of "hypochondria of the heart" is one of the most distinctive and thought-provoking books I have ever read. It is also beautifully written. You could do much worse than buy or borrow a copy, especially if you happen to be Ray Davies.

Select Kinks Discography
1966 — 1969

UK Kinks singles	Catalogue number	Release date
'Sunny Afternoon' / 'I'm Not Like Everybody Else'	Pye 7N 17125	June 3rd 1966
'Dead End Street' / 'Big Black Smoke'	Pye 7N 17222	November 18th 1966
'Waterloo Sunset' / 'Act Nice And Gentle'	Pye 7N 17321	May 5th 1967
'Autumn Almanac' / 'Mister Pleasant'	Pye 7N 17400	October 13th 1967
'Wonderboy' / 'Polly'	Pye 7N 17468	April 5th 1968
'Days' / 'She's Got Everything'	Pye 7N 17573	June 28th 1968
'Plastic Man' / 'King Kong'	Pye 7N 17724	March 28th 1969

UK Dave Davies singles		
'Death Of A Clown' / 'Love Me Till The Sun Shines'	Pye 7N 17356	July 7th 1967
'Susannah's Still Alive' / 'Funny Face'	Pye 7N 17429	November 24th 1967
'Lincoln County' / 'There Is No Life Without Love'	Pye 7N 17514	August 30th 1968
'Hold My Hand' / 'Creeping Jean'	Pye 7N 17678	January 17th 1969

UK albums

Face To Face	Pye N(S)PL 18149	October 28th 1966
Something Else By The Kinks	Pye N(S)PL 18193	September 15th 1967
Live At Kelvin Hall	Pye N(S)PL 18191	January 12th 1968
The Kinks Are The Village Green Preservation Society	Pye N(S)PL 18233	November 22nd 1968
Arthur Or The Decline And Fall Of The British Empire	Pye N(S)PL 18317	October 10th 1969

All the above titles were reissued on CD by Essential! Records in 1998 in mono editions, most with extra tracks.

Other notable releases

The Kink Kronikles	Reprise 2XS 6454	March 25th 1972
The Great Lost Kinks Album	Reprise MS 2127	January 25th 1973
BBC Sessions 1964–1967	Sanctuary SANDD010	March 12th 2001

The Kink Kronikles and *BBC Sessions 1964–1967* are available on CD. As detailed above, many tracks from *The Great Lost Kinks Album* and Dave Davies' unreleased solo album are currently only available on bootleg.

———

Notes

As a result of the changing ownership of the Pye catalogue over the last thirty years, much of the Pye Studios documentation relating to The Kinks' recordings from 1966 to 1969 has been either lost or destroyed. All discographical and recording data is taken from *You Really Got Me: An Illustrated World Discography Of The Kinks, 1964–1993* by Doug Hinman with Jason Brabazon (Rock 'n' Roll Research Press, 1994), the standard Kinks' reference work and a truly magnificent feat of diligence and research. Where recording dates are not known, I have followed Hinman's 'best guess'.

Given the variations that occur between sleeve and label on the original *TKATVGPS*, I have preferred titles as they appear on the album's most recent reissue, Essential! Records, Castle Communications Plc., 1998.

Unless noted, all quotes are from interviews conducted by the author between October 2002 and March 2003.

[i]*Disc and Music Echo*, Penny Valentine, November 4th 1967
[ii]Jon Savage, unpublished interview, 1984
[iii]*X-Ray*, Ray Davies, Pg 356
[iv]*Disc and Music Echo*, August 1966
[v]*Goldmine*, Ken Sharp, 1996
[vi]*RockBill*, Mike Hammer, May 1988
[vii]*Disc and Music Echo*, August 1966
[viii]*X-Ray*, Ray Davies, Pg 361
[ix]*Mojo 21*, August 1995
[x]*The Kinks, The Official Biography*, Jon Savage, Pg 101

———

[xi]*Kink, An Autobiography*, Dave Davies, Pg 107
[xii]*Record Mirror*, Feb 4th 1967
[xiii]Ibid.
[xiv]Jon Savage, unpublished interview, 1984
[xv]*NME*, May 13th 1967
[xvi]Ibid.,
[xvii]*NME*, May 20th 1967
[xviii]*The Story Of The Kinks*, Virgin Video, 1987
[xix]*NME*, May 20th 1967
[xx]*Rave*, November 1967
[xxi]*Rave*, September 1967
[xxii]Dave Davies interviewed by Alan Walsh, *Melody Maker*, August 12th 1967
[xxiii]*Rave*, August 1967
[xxiv]Dave Davies interviewed by Bob Farmer, *Disc and Music Echo*, July 8th 1967
[xxv]*The Story Of The Kinks*, Virgin Video, 1987
[xxvi]*Mojo* 111, Peter Doggett, February 2003
[xxvii]*Melody Maker*, October 21st 1967
[xxviii]*Disc and Music Echo*, November 11th 1967
[xxix]*Sunday Express*, Chris Goodman, April 28th 2002
[xxx]*Rolling Stone*, November 10th 1969
[xxxi]Kinks Fan Club Magazine, 2001
[xxxii]Interview with John C. Falstaff, May 3rd 1998
[xxxiii]*Music Connection*, Carla Hay, November 10th 1996
[xxxiv]Kinks Fan Club Magazine, 2001
[xxxv]*Disc and Music Echo*, February 10th 1968
[xxxvi]*Melody Maker*, August 24th 1968
[xxxvii]*X-Ray*, Ray Davies, Pg 360
[xxxviii]Ibid.,
[xxxix]Kinks Fan Club Magazine, June 1999
[xl]*Kink, An Autobiography*, Dave Davies, Pg 108
[xli]*Melody Maker*, Chris Welch, June 29th 1968

[xlii]*Melody Maker*, July 6th 1968
[xliii]*Melody Maker*, August 3rd 1968
[xliv]*Disc and Music Echo*, August 3rd 1968
[xlv]*New Musical Express*, August 3rd 1968
[xlvi]*Melody Maker*, August 24th 1968
[xlvii]*New Musical Express*, August 31st 1968
[xlviii]*X-Ray*, Ray Davies, Pg 361
[xlix]*Melody Maker*, August 3rd 1968
[l]*Disc and Music Echo*, November 23rd 1968
[li]BBC Radio 1, November 26th 1968
[lii]*Melody Maker*, November 30th 1968
[liii]Ibid.,
[liv]*Rolling Stone*, November 10th 1969
[lv]Jon Savage, unpublished interview, 1984
[lvi]*Village Voice*, April 10th 1969
[lvii]*Record Mirror*, May 10th 1969
[lviii]*Coming Up For Air*, George Orwell, Pg 30
[lix]Ibid., Pg 107
[lx]Ibid., Pg 205–207
[lxi]*Melody Maker*, November 30th 1968
[lxii]Ibid.,
[lxiii]*This Is Where I Belong: The Songs Of Ray Davies & The Kinks*, Ryko, 2002
[lxiv]Kinks Fan Club Magazine, 2001
[lxv]*Kink, An Autobiography*, Dave Davies, Pg 11
[lxvi]*Record Mirror*, October 28th 1967
[lxvii]*Melody Maker*, November 30th 1968
[lxviii]*Disc and Music Echo*, August 3rd 1968
[lxix]*Rolling Stone*, November 10th 1969
[lxx]*X-Ray*, Ray Davies, Pg 119
[lxxi]*Disc and Music Echo*, June 1965
[lxxii]*Melody Maker*, November 30th 1968
[lxxiii]*The Kinks, The Official Biography*, Jon Savage, Pg 101–102

[lxiv]*This Is Where I Belong: The Songs Of Ray Davies & The Kinks*, Ryko, 2002
[lxv]Jon Savage, unpublished interview, 1984
[lxvi]Ibid.,
[lxvii]*Goldmine*, Ken Sharp, 1996
[lxviii]*Melody Maker*, November 30th 1968
[lxix]Ibid.,
[lxx]*Melody Maker*, August 12th 1967
[lxxi]*Arena: The Orson Welles Story*, BBC, 1982
[lxxii]*The Kinks, The Official Biography*, Jon Savage, Pg 101
[lxxiii]*This Is Where I Belong: The Songs Of Ray Davies And The Kinks*, Ryko, 2002
[lxxiv]*Melody Maker*, November 30th 1968
[lxxv]*Village Voice*, April 10th 1969
[lxxvi]*The Onion a.v. club*, January 23rd 2002
[lxxvii]*Rave*, October 1967
[lxxviii]Pete Quaife interviewed by Chris Welch, *Melody Maker*, Nov 11th 1967
[lxxix]*X-Ray*, Ray Davies, Pg 369
[xc]Ibid., Pg 378
[xci]*Melody Maker*, November 30th 1968
[xcii]*Mojo* 111, February 2003
[xciii]Ibid.,
[xciv]*Melody Maker*, November 30th 1968
[xcv]*Crawdaddy*, Mark Breyer and Rik Vittenson
[xcvi]*Rolling Stone*, Loraine Alterman, December 18th 1969
[xcvii]*Crawdaddy*, Mark Breyer and Rik Vittenson
[xcviii]*X-Ray*, Ray Davies, Pg 329
[xcix]*The Mojo Collection*, 2000, Pg 161
[c]*X-Ray*, Ray Davies, Pg 329
[ci]*The Kinks, The Official Biography*, Jon Savage, Pg 106
[cii]*X-Ray*, Ray Davies, Pg 378
[ciii]*Record Collector* 169, September 1993

[civ]Jon Savage, unpublished interview, 198

[cv]Ibid.,

[cvi]*X-Ray*, Ray Davies, Pg 360

[cvii]Ibid.,

[cviii]Quoted in *The Kinks, The Sound And The Fury*, Johnny Rogan, 1984

[cix]*The Kinks, The Official Biography*, Jon Savage, Pg 104

[cx]Jon Savage, unpublished interview, 1984

[cxi]*Record Mirror*, Lon Goddard, August 1968

[cxii]Jon Savage, unpublished interview, 1984

[cxiii]*Melody Maker*, April 12th 1969

[cxiv]*NME*, April 5th 1969

[cxv]*Melody Maker*, April 12th 1969

[cxvi]*The Kinks, The Official Biography*, Jon Savage, Pg 10

[cxvii]*Beat Instrumental*, February 1969

[cxviii]*Melody Maker*, April 12th 1969

[cxix]*Record Mirror*, May 10th 1969

[cxx]*Rolling Stone*, November 1st 1969

[cxxi]*Mojo* 111, February 2003

[cxxii]*Record Collector* 169, September 1993

Big Sky contains some of the most beautiful, thunderous music The Kinks ever recorded, aligned to a vulnerability and warmth no other group – and I mean no other group – could ever hope to equal. It is a perfectly balanced production. On the one hand, the mesh of clattering drums and electric guitar never threatens to overwhelm the melody; on the other, the gossamer-light harmonies, Ray and Dave's vocal line traced by Rasa Davies' wordless falsetto, are bursting with emotion. When most of the instruments drop away at 1.20, the effect is effortlessly vivid – two lines where Davies' performance is both nonchalant and impassioned. The result is wonderfully, enchantingly sad, made more so perhaps by the knowledge that The Kinks will never again sound so refined or so right.

Ignored by virtually everyone upon its release in November 1968, *The Kinks Are The Village Green Preservation Society* is now seen as one of the best British albums ever recorded. Here, Andy Miller traces the perilous circumstances surrounding its creation, and celebrates the timeless, perfectly crafted songs pieced together by a band who were on the verge of disintegration and who refused to follow fashion.

Andy Miller is a writer living in London. His first book, *Tilting at Windmills*, was published in the UK by Viking in 2002.

US: **$9.95**
UK: **£6.99**

continuum
NEW YORK • LONDON
www.continuumbooks.com

ISBN 0-8264-1498-2

90000

9 780826 414984